# This book is f

- You are new to Network Marketing

- You have been involved in Direct Selling and Network Marketing for a while and want practical knowledge to accelerate your growth

- You want a hands-on guide to help your downline understand Direct Selling and Network Marketing to a better degree

- You want tried and tested practical know-how to get the top of your company

- You want mindset strategies to help propel you to the next level

# Dedication

This book is dedicated to my mum, whom without years of nurture and support, I would not be the person and leader I am today. Mum, I thank you and love you very much.

# About the author

Yogeeta offers 19 years of experience in Direct Sales, with an illustrious 16 of those years in Network Marketing. This has made her a sought-after leader, trainer and coach within the industry. She has a passion for training, inspiring leading and making a difference within the lives of others.

Yogeeta is known for being a highly inspirational and motivational leader and coach within the Network Marketing industry. In her own charismatic, off-the-cuff and inimitable style, she has motivated and inspired countless people within her organisation, including many leaders. Yogeeta also offers her support to anyone else who wants to make a difference. She possesses the magical ability to reignite people's enthusiasm and help them move from where they are, to where they want to be.

After finding herself in nearly £33k of debt in 2006 and losing nearly everything in January 2007, using Law of Attraction techniques, Yogeeta has turned her life around through Network Marketing and gone on to build a business that has sold nearly £9m at the time of writing, getting to the top of her company in the process. She continues to attract public relation and media attention, having been featured in many newspapers and magazines regarding her success.

# About the author

She has recently also collaborated as a co-author in 'A View from the TOP', an inspirational book dedicated to successful women within the Direct Selling Industry.

She continues to build her career with passion and vigour.

www.facebook.com/yogeetamistryonline

and also

www.directsellingsuccess.co.uk

www.facebook.com/directsellingsuccess

# Visit my website!

## Would you like some pure gold?

If you are finding this book helpful and would like to learn more, I have prepared some additional material, including some video training material, as a **FREE GIFT** from me to you. Just visit www.directsellingsuccess.co.uk and follow the links. You will also find out there about my blog, my hints and tips newsletter, as well as the live events I'll be speaking at. Enjoy!

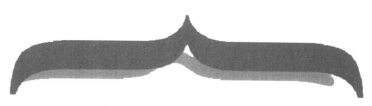

*"There are no limits to
our opportunities.
Most of us only see a small
portion of what is possible.
We create opportunities by
seeing possibilities,
and having the persistence
to act upon them.*

*We must always remember.....
opportunities are always here, but we must
look for them."*

# Direct

# Selling

# Success

by

## Yogeeta Mistry

Published by
Filament Publishing Ltd
16, Croydon Road, Waddon,
Croydon, Surrey CR0 4PA
Telephone +44 (0) 20 8688 2598
Email: info@filamentpublishing.com
Website: www.filamentpublishing.com

ISBN  978-1-908691-43-9

Printed by Berforts Information Press, Stevenage & Hastings

# Contents

*"The people who get on in this world are the people who get up and look for the circumstances they want, and if they can't find them, make them."*

**George Bernard Shaw**

# Foreword

I can remember back in 1996, when I joined my first Network Marketing company, how nervous I was with my new business kit, manual and tools, reading through the literature, watching the company video (remember the VCR?), soaking up all the success stories and wondering how, and if, I would ever be that successful. "Can I do this?" I would question myself.

I was sold with the concept of Network Marketing as soon as it was presented to me and wondered when my dreams of having an amazing lifestyle would turn into reality. I recall my first opportunity meeting, looking around the room, almost star-struck, meeting the high flyers and the living, breathing success stories I had read about and watched within the company literature, hoping that one day I would be the next big thing that everyone would be talking about. "How did they do it?" I would question myself. "How are they so successful?"

I was *hungry* for information, *eager* to get my hands on any scrap of information that would take me to the next level.

The people around me always said the best way to be successful is by following success and learning from other people's experiences, rather than trying to learn from your own trial and error. Someone else has usually failed and then got it right!

So, why take the long route and make the mistakes yourself? I was continually hunting out information in books and personal development programmes to *help me* build my Network Marketing business and recruit more people.

Now, 16 years on from the time I first dipped my toe into the world of Direct Sales, here's my gift to you: all of my years of experience and knowledge packed into 21 bite-sized chunks to hopefully make an impact and help you grow your business bigger, stronger and better. I want you to use this book almost like a universal business manual that is an extension to your starter kit or business manual that you can refer to time and again.

Let me tell you a little bit about my journey. 2012 has seen me embark on my sixteenth year within the Direct Selling industry, and I have been living and breathing it for all of these years. Some of the early years were not so successful; in 2006, I was living in rented accommodation, trying to cope with debts of over £33,000, struggling to pay the bills, driving a second hand car with not much positive visualisation for my future.

However, through belief, drive, intention and purpose, the latter years have given me the success I was looking for.

I'm sure it's comforting to hear that I've had failures as well as successes; it's been by no means plain sailing for me and I wasn't the entrepreneur I am today; I have truly evolved.

At the time of writing, I have successfully built up a business that turned over £2.4m in 2012, £8.7m in total to date, and have built a fantastic income living an enviable lifestyle. By joining the right company *for me*, and through hard work and dedication, I have turned my life around. I haven't actually retired from my business either to impart what I've learned, and very much actively build my business with vigour and passion by myself, no partner, and have done so for years. Everything I offer in this book is experience gained at first hand, which is powerful.

I am quite straight-talking and no-nonsense in my approach – just to warn you! But, if something resonates within you, then it's that very thing you have to pay attention to and possibly make a change to. If something you read makes you feel slightly uncomfortable, then that's what you need to change. If you want things to change on the outside, then the inside must change first.

So, before I share with you my 21 Keys to unlocking Direct Selling Success, let me share my mantra with you:

### *"In order for success to happen, you have to expect it first."*

*Yogeeta*

"The things that are easy to do,
are also easy not to do.
That's the difference between
Success and failure,
pennies and fortune."

Jim Rohn

# Introduction

D irect Selling is usually something that finds you, am I right? It certainly was for me. You may have not actively gone out there looking for a Direct Selling company to join.

In many cases (and your situation may be like this), you may have just simply stumbled across it; a small business card; an advert on a notice board, a friend of yours may have mentioned it – but usually you would never have contemplated the idea. It's usually only once you have joined a Direct Selling company you realise the potential of what it can offer, and then opens up endless possibilities!

Whichever company you are involved with, the fundamental principles of Direct Selling and team building are basically the same and it all fits into the bigger umbrella of Direct Sales. Simply if you're offering a product or service directly to an end user, and if you're recruiting others to do the same, you're involved in Direct Sales.

Therefore, it doesn't matter which company you're involved with, how your company is structured, how your commission or compensation plan works – you're operating within this 'umbrella' of Direct Sales, hence the title of my book, *Direct Selling Success*.

This is a book with generic *hands-on advice* that you can implement immediately into your business. I am going to share with you my secrets and impart valuable experience and knowledge that has taken me the last 16 years to gain.

I've tried new ideas and I've failed at others, so I can safely say what to do and definitely what *not* to do! I have a passion for training, inspiring and helping those around me get the results they want, and I'm hoping that after you have read this, it will give you inspiration along with the *practical* know-how and the encouragement to help make a difference in your business.

I am going to share with you important strategy and mindset principles that I feel are crucial factors to helping you with your Direct Selling Success.

The information is current, it's fresh, it's generic to whichever company you are involved with and you will find that some of it will resonate within you to help you understand and run your Direct Selling business to a better degree.

Here are just a few reading guidelines. For simplicity, throughout this book I'm going to use the term Direct Sales or Direct Selling in a generic sense to refer to our industry; whether you're involved with Party Plan, Referral Marketing, a service-based company, Network Marketing, Multi-level Marketing, our industry is Direct Sales.

I will also use the term Distributor generically to refer to *you* and your team; in your company you may be a consultant, a representative, a leader, a party plan organiser, and so forth. So disregard whatever terminology your company uses and when I say Distributor, I mean *you* and your team members.

One last tip: please read the book with a highlighter pen, or keep a pencil to hand.

If something really resonates within you, highlight the page for ease of reference. Don't worry about scribbling all over the book – look at it like a business manual. These are your guidelines for success and when you have inspired thought, capture it, make a note, keep reference and write things down. So, let's begin your journey to Direct Selling Success!

"Look for your choices,
pick the best one,
then go with it."
Pat Riley

# Key 1

## Why have you chosen Direct Selling?

This first of my 21 Keys may be more relevant to those of you that may be dipping your toe for the first time into this industry, the beginners. As I mentioned in my introduction, like myself, you may have stumbled across Direct Sales.

Maybe you heard about it through word of mouth – a friend or a relative – which is the best way to market your business initially in my opinion! Or you may have seen an advertisement in your local newspaper, or seen an advert online.

What I'm trying to say is that often, Direct Sales finds you – you don't really go out there looking for it necessarily. It's usually a void in your life that prompts you to take action and you notice adverts that you may have seen many times before, or begin to pay attention to a friend that has been telling you about their business for months! Sound familiar?

This void more often than not is of a monetary nature, but opportunities usually come floating into your life at the right time and we become more perceptive.

However, in some cases, and this may be true to you, you may have wanted to simply cure boredom and looked for something to do, meet new people, have another interest or heard about a fantastic product that you wanted to try. It is rare that someone specifically seeks out a certain Direct Sales company to join, that is, unless you have been involved in a company before and know what you are looking for.

So, if you're a complete beginner reading, you'll probably know nothing about Direct Selling and building your own team and this whole industry will feel like you're venturing into unchartered waters.

## Why have you joined?

First things first: you are about to embark on, or may have already joined, your first Direct Sales company. Now you know a little bit about the company that you've joined, why have you made this choice?  What has 'turned you on' to it? Is it extra money? Is it a new career? Are you wanting to replace an income?

It's important that you know **<u>why</u>** you've joined and what appeals to you – this is where your drive and enthusiasm will come from.

> *"With a big enough reason 'why'*
> *you  want to do something,*
> *the 'how to'  becomes easy."*

If you've never been involved in a Direct Selling environment before, then essentially you'll be doing one of two things or both straight away: recommending the product or service, producing retail sales and offering an opportunity for others to join your team. So, if you are brand new to all of this: Welcome to the Direct Selling Industry!

## Industry 'Unwritten' Rules

There is an unwritten rule in Direct Sales I would like you to grasp straight away, and that is Direct Sales is a numbers game. The more you offer your product, service or opportunity, the more you increase your chances of success. In the early days, what you lack in skill you can make up in numbers.

What do I mean by that?  Well, a seasoned distributor in this industry with years of experience can speak to less people and make more sales and sponsor or recruit more. If you're new, you can, with raw enthusiasm, produce exactly the same results if you speak to twice as many people as the seasoned distributor!

Consider it a fact of the Direct Selling world. The more you do, the better results you'll get.

The less you do, the less likely you are to produce results; it stands to reason.

***"An important rule to remember is the more you do, or the harder you work, the luckier you will get."***

Which in other words means, the more you offer your product or service, the more chances you'll get buyers or takers. And the more you offer the opportunity for others to join you, the more new recruits you'll find. Unfortunately, rejection goes hand in hand with this and you may not be used to getting rejected.

Nobody likes rejection, let's face it! The word 'No' is the hardest word to swallow. Here's a tip: don't take 'No's' personally.

It is not you they are rejecting, simply the product or the business you are offering. The more 'No's' you get simply means that you're getting closer to more 'Yes's'. Now, I never *fully* understood this phrase when I was new in this industry and I would hear people say this at training sessions. "How on earth," I would contemplate to myself, "can more 'No's' mean there is a 'Yes' around the corner?" It's called Law of Averages and understanding this is key to your ongoing development. People have different attitudes, opinions, values, mindset, beliefs and circumstances. You're just trying to find those who 'fit' with what you've got to offer. So, let's say you line up 10 people in a parade. You could offer your business, get 10 'No's' in a row and that's it, game over. If you did the same, but this time you lined up one hundred people, you have given yourself more scope. This time, after 10 or 20 'No's, likelihood is that someone will 'fit' with what you're offering and you'll get a few 'Yes's' - that is the Law of Averages.

Learn to embrace rejection – it's normal and it just brings you closer to the Yes's that you want! How much rejection have you had so far in your business? Not a lot? Quite a bit?

If you've not had a lot of rejection, then you're doing something wrong! I'm here to tell you that it's normal to get 'No's'.

However, I also know how difficult it is to palate when someone says no to you – oh, how such a small word can hurt!

*"I've missed more than 9,000 shots in my career.*
*I've lost nearly 300 games.*
*26 times I've been trusted to take the game*
*winning shot and missed.*
*I've failed over and over again in my life.*
*And that's why I succeed".*

**Michael Jordan, Pro Basketball player**

There are, of course, other skills you will develop along the way, especially if you aspire to create a substantial income and career out of your Direct Selling business. However, it all starts with the basics of recommending the product or service and producing retail sales.

## So where do I fit?

It's very important that you know exactly why you've chosen this industry and where you fit into it. Your eyes usually get opened up to the possibilities after you've joined and completed your first few weeks and months.

I know that my desire was ignited to grow a massive team and make my business work when I was invited to a Business Opportunity meeting where I saw the leaders within my company and listened to their journey on the ladder of success from a level playing field.

You will probably fall into one of the three types of people below that join our industry and *it really doesn't matter* which one you fall into. It all depends on your personal circumstances and your level of ambition.

Just understand where you are and what you want:

1.    Part-time income seeker
2.    Full-time income seeker
3.    Business builder

## Part-time income seeker

You may be in full- or part-time employment and are looking for a way to supplement your income. Or you may be new to your area and looking to meet new people, a new parent looking to fill some spare time, or retired but looking to stay active.

You are happy in your current situation whatever that may be, you don't necessarily want to change your current situation in any drastic way and merely wish to enhance your current lifestyle.

You don't want to give up your job, as you may be happy with this, or find a new career, and you don't have the desire to build a substantial business, so long as your Direct Selling business fills a need.

You don't have a great sense of urgency to build your business quickly as it is not priority and you are content to pace yourself. *Is this you?*

## Full-time income seeker

You would like to be able to work from home and build a full-time income, whatever a full-time income means to you.

You may not have a job or career that satisfies you, or you may currently not be in a full-time job or career, hence your wish to build up a full-time income with your business.

Or you may be in an unhappy job or career and looking to replace this income so you can work for yourself.

You are prepared to work hard at it within usually limited part-time hours - you may be a full-time parent with limited time around the children or you may be working full-time and building an income part-time in limited hours.

It is priority to build your business as you may be dissatisfied within your current situation so there is significant importance placed on your business, however you know you have time constraints so you are aware that building your business will take time. However, your Direct Selling business has significant importance in your life. *Is this you?*

## Business builder

You are a serious from day one. You know *exactly* what you want from your business and you are in it for the long haul.

You have had a 'do whatever it takes' attitude towards your business from day one and your business will come first before most things. You are prepared to work seven days per week and burn the candle at both ends in order to get the momentum up to where you need to get your business growing. Your situation bears no relevance and you are prepared to eat, sleep and drink your business to get it up and running as fast as you can! *Is this you?*

Do any of these ring true to you? You will fit into one of these categories. What I would like to emphasise is that it doesn't matter at all which one you fit into; we are all different and made up differently and join Direct Selling for different reasons.

Whichever category you feel you fit into, then understand it as this will determine how much time and effort you want to dedicate. Of course, your circumstances may change and you may change direction, but the point I am trying to make is that *it doesn't matter what someone else tells you where you need to be* – understand **your own** set of circumstances and work to this. If you want to change direction and devote more time and effort, then upgrade your commitment level, by all means.

You can choose to work as hard as you want, or choose to take your foot off the pedal – it all boils down to you and your motivations. We are all alike, as well as different, and what you want from your Direct Selling business is ultimately up to you, but *never let anyone dictate the speed at which you want to build your business* and the levels you desire to attain. Your business is your creation and it is up to you what levels you aspire to.

Whatever you have decided that your schedule is, make the promise to yourself and work to the levels you have set out for yourself.

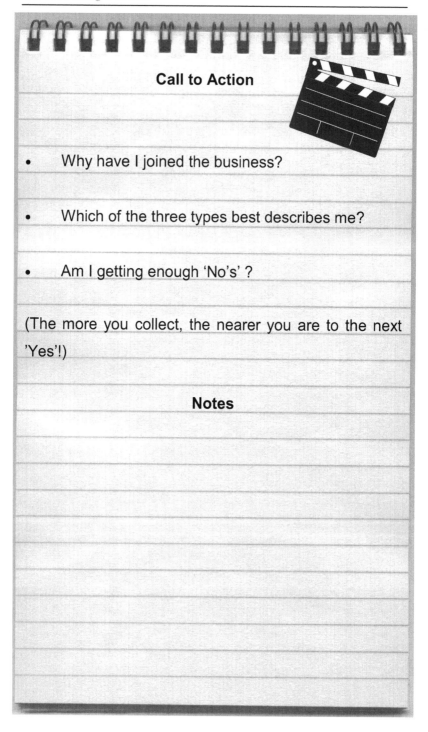

**Call to Action**

- Why have I joined the business?

- Which of the three types best describes me?

- Am I getting enough 'No's' ?

(The more you collect, the nearer you are to the next 'Yes'!)

**Notes**

*"If you are not financially
independent by the time
you are forty or fifty,
it doesn't mean that you are
living in the wrong country
or at the wrong time.
It simply means that you
have the wrong plan."*

**Jim Rohn**

"*Diligence is the mother
of good fortune.*"
Benjamin Disraeli

# Key 2

## Do your research!

Imagine this scenario – you've woken up one morning and decided you want to buy a franchise. What's the first thing you're going to do? Are you going to rush to the bank, spend thousands of your own money or borrow thousands on the first franchise you find?

Or do you think you would go online and do some research, read some journals, visit some shows, have a few meetings with franchisors and get some questions answered before you decide to commit yourself?

Wouldn't it be sensible to first find a sector that you have an interest in, or maybe even some experience in, and I'm sure you would want to find out how profitable that business sector is and how great a demand there is for the product or service being offered.

Before committing thousands of your hard-earned cash into a franchise, you'd do a lot of market research and conduct your due diligence, wouldn't you agree?

You certainly wouldn't jump into it feet first without batting an eyelid, that's for sure!

The Direct Sales company that you choose to become involved with, I feel, is of *paramount* importance. It's certainly a recipe for success if you find a company and a product that you *really believe in* and fits with your values. This is the first step on your ladder to Direct Selling Success.

In my opinion, you cannot join your company simply because someone has convinced or persuaded you that it's the best thing since sliced bread! If you're feeling half-hearted about a particular opportunity that is being presented to you, then don't join that particular company. Simply find something else that fits with you.

I was young when I joined my first Direct Sales company, a well-known Network Marketing company. A colleague of mine presented an opportunity to me. I do recall I was hooked with the Network Marketing concept immediately, helping others and creating a team and the long-term residual income it can provide.

However, I wasn't completely sure that the opportunity being presented was the *right* company for me, although I really was sold on the concept. Hastily, without having the common sense to conduct my own due diligence, (and, by the way, common sense isn't common!) I jumped into that particular company, albeit with trepidation and a bit of doubt.

Suffice to say, I just could not progress within that company because it wasn't a 'heart' decision for me. What do I mean? It just didn't feel right from the start. As much as I tried, I couldn't learn to 'love' what I was doing.

This is definitely not a recipe for success. It was, in fact, several years later when I made some decisions, started researching and spent a few months asking questions, contacting distributors, looking at the commission structures of different companies, that I found a company that 'fit' what I was looking for.

If you are feeling a little doubtful about the company that you're involved with, then you need to make certain choices and make some changes.

**Live your life by the 3 Cs:**
**Choice, Chance and Change:**
**You must make the Choice,**
**to take the Chance**
**if you want anything to Change**

If you feel that you are not fulfilling your potential and you're not earning what you really want, or, if you're not feeling as enthusiastic about what you're representing, be bold enough to find something that you feel passionately about. Life is not going to wait for you!

Passion ignites enthusiasm, and enthusiasm will drive you and keep that burning desire inside to want to work at your business. Become involved with a Direct Selling company and stay involved because you *WANT* to, because it *feels right* FOR YOU and because you believe totally in what you're doing!

If it doesn't feel right, then it's not right for you. Once you choose the right company for you, you'll fly to the levels that you personally aspire to because you'll be building your business with the *conviction* you need. Success cannot happen with doubt, only conviction.

# Here's a checklist

Do you:

- Have a passion for the product or service being offered?

- Love the company philosophy?

- Want to talk about your company to everyone you meet?

- Feel enthusiastic to work at your business every day?

Does it:

- Fit with your lifestyle and ethics?

Can you:

- Feel that you can be successful with it?

- Feel that you are providing a benefit to others by them joining you?

Some distributors may disagree with me about choosing the right company but if you love what you're representing, how can you go wrong?

They say the product doesn't matter, it's the commission plan, but let's look at it this way; you could have the best commission plan in the world but if you're selling bicycles for fish, then I have a sneaky suspicion you're not going to make a lot of money from it!

> *"We can have more than we've*
> *got because we can become*
> *more than we are."*
> **Jim Rohn**

## Call to Action

- Have I done my research thoroughly?

- Do I really feel enthusiastic about what it is that I will be selling?

- Do be honest with yourself!

- Does it fit with my life and my ethics?

- Do I feel comfortable talking to anyone about it?

## Notes

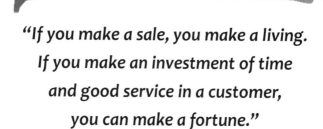

"If you make a sale, you make a living.
If you make an investment of time
and good service in a customer,
you can make a fortune."
Jim Rohn

# Key 3

## Making retail sales

This is something I feel very passionately about, and that's building a strong, customer base. Selling the products or service is the foundation of your business.

Your initial source of income will be generated from offering the product or service you're representing and is an important 'cog' in the business wheel of your success. All Direct Selling companies operate on a similar basis: Retail, Recruit, Teach.

Therefore, the retail aspect is an integral part of what you do. Here is something I've heard many times before: "I don't want to sell the product/service, I just want to sponsor/recruit others!"

Imagine if Tesco had the same philosophy – they would have a shop floor full of staff with shelves full of product, but no customers in the store! The sale of a product or service is the life blood of ANY business, anywhere in the world. Think about that for a minute.

You cannot expect anyone in your Direct Selling business to do something that you haven't done yourself. And if you haven't done it yourself, you cannot possibly teach someone else to do it. Learn to do the retail part of your business well and then simply teach what you do well to your new distributors and this is a recipe for a strong business. If you build a strong customer base, others in your team will follow you.

There are two types of Direct Selling companies:

- product-driven – where there is a tangible product
- service-based – usually offering utilities, anything that is intangible

Whether you've chosen a product-driven or service-based company, both require a strong customer base in order for any uptake of the product or service. Before I give you selling tips, first and foremost, you've got to believe in the product or service that you're selling, which I covered in Key 2. I do hope you've put some thought in choosing the company that you're involved with. If you've chosen your company carefully, then offering the product or service should be something you're feeling really enthusiastic about and feel at ease doing.

On the other hand, if you're feeling reluctant and not very enthusiastic about offering your product or service then there's a problem and there is no point trying to 'convince' yourself you're feeling positive about it – you either do or you don't. If it doesn't feel right, you won't want to talk about it and you definitely won't be finding any customers or making any sales! You can 'fake it till you make it' but it's hard work; believe me, I've been there! There's nothing worse than trying to promote or sell something that you're almost embarrassed to represent as there will be a distinct lack of enthusiasm and passion required to get the kick-start you need. Ensure what you're selling and recommending fits with you, your values and your lifestyle. Go with your gut feeling. If it feels right, then it's a match and you'll begin to experience success straight away.

## Using the products

Within product-driven businesses, some Direct Selling companies do promote that you use the products to feel the benefits of them so that you can effectively recommend them to others. That is fine and I will always encourage you to use the product or service that you are offering and for you to be your best customer. For example, you wouldn't find a Ford car salesman driving a Renault! However, my advice is be cautious: don't get yourself into a situation where all you are doing is spending money on your own personal orders every month, rather than creating sales through a base of customers. In my opinion, it defeats the object of trying to find customers if you're just purchasing stock to create personal volume every sales cycle within your company to satisfy a sales requirement, if indeed there is one. There should be product movement through a customer base. Your new business should be self-sustaining within a few weeks and if you believe in your product or service enough, you should easily be able to find customers to sell the product or service to.

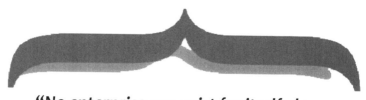

"No enterprise can exist for itself alone.
It ministers to some great need,
it performs some great service,
not for itself, but for others;
or failing therein,
it ceases to be profitable
and ceases to exist."

Calvin Coolidge

## Building your customer base is a numbers game

An important question to ask and know is to find out the optimum amount of customers you need in order to build a profitable customer base. Working towards optimums is better than working on minimums.

I mentioned earlier in Key 2 that building your business is a numbers game. For the best success for you, offer your product or service to as many people as you can. Discover the best ways to market your product or service. Are there several distribution methods? Which is the most effective method? Most likely, it will be through one of these, or a combination of the following methods:

- personal recommendation/referral
- party plan and/or demonstration
- brochure placement

For personal recommendation, your product or service needs to be seen and/or demonstrated. Ask yourself if you have enough product knowledge. If not, enrol on more training so you begin to build the foundations of expertise. Your company may even provide online training that you can complete in your own time. If so, I strongly recommend that you take the online training. Have you made a list of the people and places to whom you are going to recommend the product or service to? Where are you going to demonstrate them and how? Who can benefit from them? Are there local groups, places, markets and institutes where you can promote them? If you've gained personal benefit from your product or service, then get your testimonial out there, blog about your experiences to attract online customers and perhaps offer press releases to capture the offline audience and attract customers. Once a customer has had a positive experience of that product or service, document the testimonial, with their permission of course, and then distribute the testimonials. Social media is a great way to get positive testimonials out there. A great example of how you can use your niche to promote your product or service is to think about where it fits. For example, health care products may be great to sell at your local gym or slimming club, so ask if you can hold a demonstration there. Utilities may be better sold if you approach small business owners who need to make savings, thinking about their bottom line. Always be thinking outside of the box. You may get more sales by demonstrating at groups than purely to individuals.

If your company promotes sales though party plan, firstly enrol on training and be open to as much product knowledge and information as possible. There is nothing worse than feeling unprepared! The more you learn about your product, the benefits, what makes you different and why people will want your product, the more confident you'll feel when you conduct your first parties and demonstrations. Second, be sure to have six bookings for the first two weeks. If you aim to have three bookings per week in the first two weeks, that will then give you good momentum upon which to create more bookings. It is a common trap to rely upon one or two bookings and hoping and praying that you're going to get more bookings from that first one. Ensure that at least 20 people are invited to each party (which is usually the role of the host or hostess to do, so coach your host on how to do this). If you invite 20, then approximately 10 will turn up on the day. Always remember it's safety in numbers. To have one hundred percent attendance is rare and you will have no shows on the day so please try not to get too dismayed by this. As I mentioned before, rejection is part and parcel of Direct Sales and is an aspect to accept. Think outside the box with parties too: where will you have a captive audience for your product? Think about community groups, local social groups, gatherings, ladies nights at your child's school, fetes, fundraisers; the possibilities are endless once you get thinking.

*TOP TIP! Always write things down. When you get new ideas or inspired thought, write things down. Here's a good phrase: Feeling listless? Then make a list!*

Does your company use brochure placement or catalogues? If so, the key here is to distribute these to as many people, places, institutes and businesses as you can. One or two catalogues won't get you an abundance of orders. On the other hand, how far will hundred of catalogues get you? Go business to business and door to door. The less time you leave your brochures or catalogues, the more urgency the potential customer will have to place an order so the trick here is to give them as little time as possible to look at your material, usually around 48 hours, sometimes even the same day. Don't base your decisions on early results here. People's buying habits and patterns differ and often it's continuity of seeing the same catalogue before they commit to becoming a customer. There are also other components and deciding factors here: the build-up of trust between you and the prospective customer. Have they the time to look at your material. Have they got the cash flow to make a purchase? Often, someone may need to see a catalogue several times before finally deciding to buy and becoming a customer. Looking for results immediately will lead to you feeling rather dejected. Rather, focus on building up your brand, your reputation and trust with prospective customers.

Let me reiterate: rejection and selling go hand in hand.

No matter which method you are using to promote your product or service, the key to everything I'm saying here is safety in numbers. Marketing is about getting the word out there. I've seen many distributors try and be secret agents and think that they are going make sales. Don't be a secret agent – leave that to 007! ;)

## C.A.R.E.
## Customers Are Really Everything

If you need advice about your products or service, ask for advice and get along to some training meetings which tell you about the benefits of the product or service you are offering. If there are competitor products or services on the market, then do your due diligence and go on a fact find about rival products or services. It makes perfect business sense to do this so you can best promote what you have to offer. Do ensure you have a sound understanding about your own product or service and find the USP – Unique Selling Point. This will give you the answers as to why your product or service is better than the rivals in the marketplace. I'm not advocating that you need to become an expert overnight on your product or service which, when you're a brand new distributor, this will be a tall order. All I feel you need to do is invest a little time in learning what you have to offer to give you the best start possible.

## Don't prejudge

How can you tell by looking at someone whether they want your product or service? Well the answer is simple: you can't! If you are presented with a line-up of people and you're asked to pick out those of them who you think will want your product or service just by looking at them, do you think you could successfully pick them out? Of course not! Unless they have a label on their back saying, "Yes, please pick me!" you can't prejudge who will want your product or service and you don't know how and where you'll get your next sale. So, why have I heard so often in the past, "Oh, I really don't think she will be interested," or, "He's definitely not interested in buying my products so I'm not even going approach him!" All you should know is that you don't know until you ask. Be open-minded and talk to everyone about what you have to offer. Also learn to think outside the box as to where you can promote your products or service– fetes, fayres, Facebook, Twitter, your own website, gyms, offices, house to house, home parties/

demonstrations, trade fayres, salons, shopping centres, local high street – just keep thinking and doing. This will also be tapping into your entrepreneurial spirit and you should be having fun doing it!

## Giving up too soon

Refrain from basing your judgement on early results – this is a classic mistake many distributors make. If someone doesn't buy your product or take your service straight away, that is not a cue never to approach them again. Often, people can take time to make buying decisions. What one person might say "No" to one month, they may say "Yes" to the next month. People's buying habits vary and decisions are based on timing, need and personal circumstances. If you've had twenty people in a row say they're not interested in even looking at your product or service, that does not mean your product or service will not sell and that you should give up. The company that you've joined wouldn't be in existence if your product or service did not sell! This is a *big* lesson to learn and once you learn to understand the basics that 'No's and 'Yes's go hand in hand when you're selling, then you'll start to create the perfect mindset for building your business successfully. And if you learn to build a good strong customer base, you will get repeat business which is the best start to any Direct Sales business. So just to recap: believe in what you're selling, it's safety in numbers – the more you ask, the more customers you'll find. And please, do not take rejection personally – learn to embrace it as part and parcel of your business!

## Call to Action

- Do you love the product?

- What's the optimum customer base?

- What's the best way of selling?

- Are you guilty of prejudging your potential customers?

## Notes

"Every successful person finds
that great success lies just beyond the point
where they are convinced the idea
is not going to work."

# Key 4

## The dynamics of a Direct Selling business

Like the bamboo tree it, will take time to build your Direct Selling business. I really wish I could say that you will instantly have a perfect team of distributors and sail through the various levels of the commission structure! One of the first concepts I want you to grasp is **that there is no direct correlation between your income and your hours when building a Direct Selling business.** You may currently have, or have had in the recent past, a regular salaried job. In a job, you are swapping your input in the form of a 37-50 hour week for a weekly pay packet or monthly wage. So in effect, you're swapping time for money. On the other hand, you may be a self-employed, a sole trader. When you're a sole trader, you 'own' a job, for instance a plumber, a hairdresser, an electrician, an accountant and if you stop working, your income stops. You are still swapping your time for money because your income relates directly to time input. When you're building a Direct Selling business, you are creating your own *empire* which can create you an *independent, residual* self-sustaining income that doesn't necessarily need you there.

*The story of the bamboo tree:*

*You take a little seed, plant it, water it, and*
*fertilise it for a whole year,*
*and nothing happens.*

*The second year you water it and fertilise it,*
*and nothing happens.*

*The third year you water it and fertilise it,*
*and nothing happens.*
*How discouraging this becomes!*

*The fifth year you continue to water and*
*fertilise the seed and then - take note.*
*Sometime during the fifth year,*
*the Chinese bamboo tree sprouts*
*and grows NINETY FEET IN SIX WEEKS!*

*"I would rather earn 1% off a 100 people's efforts*
*than 100% of my own efforts."*
**Jean Paul Getty**

**All you need to do is focus time and commitment to your business in the early years.** Like with any business, the work goes into the early stages and you will invest more time and effort in the early part of your Direct Selling career. Unlike a job, your monetary return won't be proportionate to the time and effort you've invested. I know from years of being in this industry that it's the disproportionate time:income ratio that disheartens many distributors in this industry and discourages them from wanting to continue building their business. Has this, or is this happening, to you? Have you found you've dedicated far more hours and not had an equivalent monetary return? It's at this point you may feel like throwing in the towel and leaving. Don't! Please, please stick with it! It is crucial that you learn to keep the blinkers on and have the vision to see beyond the smaller commission payments in the early days and grasp that the same wind blows on all new distributors in this industry, myself included.

*"When we do more than we are paid to do,*
*eventually we will be paid more for what we do."*
**Zig Ziglar**

To broaden this concept, it is the same start for any individual starting *any* type of business. You are establishing yourself, getting yourself off the ground, and this isn't going to happen overnight. Think about the corporate ladder: how long would it take, or has it taken you, to get to the top of your career? Years? Decades? Promotion in the corporate world depends on whom else you are competing with for career ladder success and, sadly, whether your face fits. On the other hand, if you're starting a business of any description, what is it going to take? Time? Financial investment? Risk? Long hours? Effort? Relentless self-promotion? Although you're not risking major investment, when you start a Direct Selling business it's going to involve time and effort for sure. Time is your *biggest* investment. Look at the benefits: you can promote yourself whenever you want with no fear of competition or glass ceilings, unlike the career ladder, and your Direct Selling business can provide you with a *residual, passive income* which most other conventional businesses cannot provide.

## Your business is like building a house

A fantastic example I can compare your business to is the process of building a house. You can't build a house without solid foundations. The foundation of your home is what takes the time. You have to dig deep, get the foundations of that house *solid* before one brick can be laid onto it. How many times have you driven past a new housing development where nothing seems to be happening, then suddenly you see *lots* of new properties emerging seemingly overnight out of nowhere. Your Direct Selling business is exactly the same. The foundations of your business is a large and solid customer base of *regular* customers who want and need your product or service and a reliable base of distributors and leaders within your team who are also selling the product or service – such a pity this can't jump out the starter pack when we join! You have the same set of circumstances as every distributor within any company: you start with nothing – just a 'cup of ambition' as Dolly Parton says in the lyrics of her song *Nine to Five*. Everything is built from scratch.

## Your due diligence

It is very wise to do your due diligence, as mentioned before: find out what the average order size is, if you are in a product-driven network, and find out the optimum size your customer base needs to be in order to generate enough sales to give you a decent retail profit. Have a plan and a strategy to begin recruiting others and promoting yourself. What's the first milestone you need to reach in order to satisfy an income goal? Is there a system in place which recommends a certain number of distributors in your team at the first level? Find out what this is and set about working towards that. Asking these kinds of questions is the astute way to approach your business.

One of the first things to do when approaching your team building is to draw up your contact list, or warm list as we call it in the industry, and talk to others within your personal network of friends, family and associates; this is the best place to start when promoting your new opportunity. Why is it called a Warm List? Because you already know these people. You have some sort of connection, rapport and bond with that person so it's far easier to pick up the phone and talk to them.

*TOP TIP! When making your Warm List, don't make a list of people you think will be interested in joining your business, just make a list. When you approach them about your business, PICK UP THE PHONE! Talk to them. Refrain from using text and email as it's far too disengaged. Connect with people, engage over the telephone. It's the best way.*

Let's think about this: whatever business you start, the first thing you'd normally do is contact everyone in your circle of influence and network and make them aware of what it is you've started. Approach your Direct Sales business in the exact same manner. Don't prejudge anyone. Have you been guilty of doing this and not offering your opportunity because superficially, someone looks like they've 'got it good?' Two nice new shiny cars on the drive but possibly no food in the fridge! Many people earn a good living and can *still* be broke. Remember, most people live to their mean and beyond and would welcome a second income! Be sure to make a list of *every* contact you know to promote yourself, not just a list of people you *think* will be interested in joining.

There is then your cold market from where you'll be generating leads to prospect about your opportunity (which I will cover in a later chapter). The possibilities are far and wide when generating leads. Let me reiterate: this is a pure numbers game when generating prospect enquiries from a cold market until you begin to find a solid base of distributors. These distributors will then begin to duplicate what you do – build a base of regular customers offering the product or service, and so your business is now beginning to grow. Like the house, the foundations are beginning to be laid.

Some of these distributors will be good, some will be not so good. Some are going to stay and some are going to leave. One thing you *must* bear in mind is that without building a *solid* foundation, you are not going to build a self-sustaining network and this foundation may take some time to put into place. The naysayers in life will look at this and try and discourage you. You may have experienced this already when those around you try and discourage you when they don't see a return from your effort. Your effort *will* outweigh your income in the early days of building your business and unless you remain focused, these negative individuals will encourage you to leave. Learn not to pay attention to what is happening in the moment.

**Call to Action**

- Make a plan for optimum customer base

- Make a plan and find out the optimum level of distributors for the first level

- Have you prejudged anyone? If so, go back and revise your list!

**Notes**

"Right from the beginning I
believed that staying the course
was what counted.
The sheer process of attrition
would wear others down.
Them that stuck it out was
them that won."
Harrison Ford, actor

# Key 5

## Your business grows exponentially

As talked about in Key 4, in the early part of your Direct Selling business, there will be no direct correlation between your income and your effort. The prize of building a successful business is at the end of your journey, not at the beginning. When you remain focused and begin to recruit others into your business and they begin to recruit, your business will begin to grow exponentially. A linear business is when you alone are building your business. Exponential growth is multiplication of the effort of many others and as more and more people start to join your business and recruit, the larger your business grows. This is leveraging your time and it's very, very powerful. You may be putting 20 hours per week into your business. If you had a team of 10 people putting 20 hours per week into their business, you've now got 220 hours per week going into your business which you are getting paid on. Understand the FULL power of leverage...it's powerful! The best illustration I can give of exponential growth is my own Direct Selling business and the first four years of how my sales and income have grown. It's usually a three to five year plan that we talk about, so here are my first four years laid bare:

## First four years' sales growth

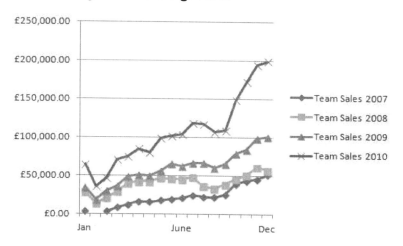

## First four years' earnings growth

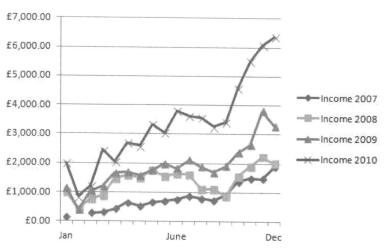

Look at the graph of my business which is based on real figures for the four years within the current Direct Sales business I have built showing my sales turnover and income, month on month, year on year, for four years. My very first commission payment for a sales cycle was a mere £30 – I can assure you that my time and fuel costs *far* outweighed that £30! But as the effort and the mental focus remained *constant*, the business began to grow; the team size increased, the time leverage increased, the sales volume increased and the income grew. The more people that joined my business, the greater that leverage became.

 ### Exponential Growth vs Multiplication

| | |
|---|---|
| 1 x 5 = 5 | 1 x 5 = 5 |
| 5 x 5 = 25 | 2 x 5 = 10 |
| 25 x 5 = 125 | 3 x 5 = 15 |
| 125 x 5 = 625 | 4 x 5 = 20 |
| 625 x 5 = 3125 | 5 x 5 = 25 |

This is the power of leverage. See how the numbers get disproportionately larger. This is exponential growth, not simply multiplication. This is how a Direct Selling business grows; there are more and more people joining your business and recruiting further down the levels.

What I *never* did was to slow down when I had a few ups and downs and that is the *biggest* mistake you can make in this industry. Slowing down momentum can cause you to slow down in the longer term and hold you back; it all has a compound effect. I never focused in the moment and kept my thoughts onto where I was headed. I knew from *day one* that I wanted a high five-figure income from my Direct Selling business within five years. There will be eventualities within your business that are unavoidable: you're going to lose customers, you're going to lose team members, you're going to have distributors who will join and let you down, or you may not find your leaders quickly enough to start getting more exponential growth. Does that mean you should quit? NO! Of course not! How many times have you failed your driving test? And did you quit? Now there were times I could easily have quit within those first six to twelve months. My personal financial situation was far from great when I was building my business with a mountain of debt to try and cope with. What kept me going was passion, focus and desire to build my business AND I accepted the realities of what was happening, but *just kept going.*

 *"Fall seven times, stand up eight."*

## Entrepreneurial time

When you are building your Direct Selling business, you are working on 'entrepreneurial' time, so there will be a shift in your mentality towards your business. Entrepreneurs do not swap time for money. They work hard for a future gain. Most, if not all, business people who run a conventional business *invest* their time and money in their business for a future return in terms of business growth and profits, which is what you are doing. Your returns are not going to be immediate. Like an entrepreneur starting in business, you are not risking your job or copious amounts of investment with your Direct Selling business. Depending on which company you've joined, it is relatively risk-free, apart from a small investment in a starter kit. Your biggest investment will be time, more than anything.

 *"Great oaks from tiny acorns grow."*

In your early days, you'll be investing time without a direct monetary return. So, I think it's really important for you to sit down with your upline, or your most successful upline who understands where you are, learn to understand your commission plan, and set a business plan for yourself along with some goals for yourself that motivate you to want to build your business. If you are working a day job, you will be in employee mode for most of the day; you will then be working on entrepreneurial time in the evening on your business, so get used to switching those 'hats'. I can imagine that this is not easy to do as you will naturally want to compare your monetary reward with your effort. Remembering this important fact in the early days of your business is sensible and as difficult as it may seem, try and refrain from feeling disheartened when the correlation between your commission from your business and your effort isn't equal. You are a budding entrepreneur of your own business and you are building the foundations of your business – learn to look at yourself like this! It's all about consistent, steady effort over a course of time and building your foundation of customers and distributors; this platform will lead you to further success.

## Something to take heed of

If anyone promises *big* money straight away, please be a little realistic and a little hesitant about joining to be perfectly frank! Direct Selling is NOT a get rich quick scheme; it's a marathon, not a sprint! Usually it will take a consistent three to five year business plan to really start to reap the rewards of building up a residual income. Take another look at the chart of what I earned. Those first few months, I was not earning the equivalent of a salary or a wage. However, look at the latter years. Success waits for those who persist, consistently. Whatever level of income you are looking for will take some time and effort, and a large profitable network will take a little while to build. Expecting a full-time income from your business immediately is a little unrealistic and I really just want you to grasp the practicalities. A sound understanding of how this business works is important so you enter into it with realistic expectations; understand the practicalities and also the realities of building a Direct Selling business.

**Call to Action**

- Learn to switch those 'hats'

- Do you know how much you want to earn in three years? Five years?

- Is your effort consistent? Learn how to stay consistent, regardless of what is happening in your business

**Notes**

"Let others leave their future in someone else's hands, but not you."

Jim Rohn

# Key 6

## Employee vs Entrepreneur - Mindset for Success

've touched on having an entrepreneurial mindset in Key 4 but I feel it's something very important so I wanted to dedicate a whole Key on it to reinforce the subject. Many of you reading are in, or have been in, salaried jobs so you are used to putting in your hours and getting a certain monetary return for those hours. If you have run your own business before or have been self-employed, you will understand devoting more time to your business in the early days without the proportionate monetary return. In a job, you are swapping your time and effort for your salary or wage at the end of the month. You are working in what I like to term as 'employee time'. However, you cannot apply the same thinking to your Direct Sales business. As soon as you join a Direct Sales company, you are working on 'entrepreneurial time' and there is never going to be a direct correlation to time and money wherever you are within your business, be that in the beginning when you're starting out or in the latter years when you're established with a big network of distributors. *You'll get paid far less for the hours that you dedicate in the early days and conversely in the latter years you'll get paid disproportionately more for the hours you put in.* The latter of these, I have to say, is a nice place to be!

This can be very tricky to deal with for the majority of you if you've not been self-employed before and if you're running your Direct Sales business alongside your full- or part-time job. You will naturally begin to compare the time you've invest into your business with the monetary gain you've had. One of the most common things I hear from new distributors is: "I've put in all these hours and I've hardly made any money...it's not worth it!" Begin today to create a new mindset and adopt a new thinking process towards your business: you are *investing* your time *now* and creating a business for a future gain and your business just gets easier the more time and effort you put in. Time is your *biggest* investment in this creation process and you need a certain degree of vision to keep you going. So, if you are running your Direct Sales business part-time, you have to leave your 'employee hat' at the office and put your 'entrepreneur hat' on as soon as you get home to run your business.

> *"The greatest tragedy in life is people who have sight, but no vision."*
> Helen Keller (1880-1968)

Refrain from putting a monetary value on your time as this is a sure-fire way to make you feel disheartened about your business. Make it a physical act: when you leave your workplace to come home, draw a mental picture of taking your employee hat off and putting your entrepreneur hat on. Have fun with it!

## Linear Income vs Exponential Income

You will be producing two types of income from your business: a linear income from your retail sales and an exponential income from your team building. The 'retail trap', as I would like to term it, can occur if you're not careful: you can often get an immediate response from your retail sales which in itself creates comfort as it's an immediate result for your time. We are too conditioned throughout life to want immediate results. Therefore, rather than going out to sponsor or recruit team members which may not always produce you instant results, you produce more retail sales to satisfy the feeling of getting more immediate results. You can then get stuck in your own comfort zone. Instant gratification is not the key to Direct Selling Success. Recruiting requires more mental stamina as often the activities you do to generate leads for new recruits may not produce an immediate result that day, or even that week. Due to this fact, you may get discouraged and remain in retail mode and slow down your recruiting efforts. Have you ever felt this way? If you have, recognise this and then make the change to remain consistent and focused with your recruiting activities, even when the results aren't showing through.

## Don't give up!

Giving up on action required to sponsor or recruit more people is a business killer. This is brought about after being too results oriented, rather than focusing on the action required. Lack of results leads to a stop/start approach, and therefore you will never gain the momentum you need to take off! It is this stop/start approach that slows far too many people down in this industry. A better approach is to remain focused on the *consistent* actions that will produce results. Be action oriented, rather than results oriented.

Let me illustrate my point with a hypothetical scenario that could happen.

You're putting in lots of effort to produce sales and recruit new distributors into your business. You're feeling really enthusiastic and working pretty hard. A few of those people leave and a few made you promises that they were going to join your team and set the world on fire, but they have fallen by the wayside and done very little to grow their business. You now begin to feel like you've taken a step backward and feel a little let down. You have a few prospects that have responded to some recruiting adverts of yours but you don't see the point in calling them – well, what's the use! You may even take a week off from your business. Your business has plateaued and this leaves you feeling a little more despondent than before that all your efforts were futile. You eventually get around to calling those prospects back that replied to your adverts, only to find that one of them was raring to get started, loved the concept, but has now joined another person's team! If only you'd stayed focused and followed up all your prospects! It's an ever decreasing circle and I think you see my point.

When the going gets tough, the tough get going! You have to learn to keep going through all the ups and downs so when things aren't going as planned, just stay focused and keep doing all the things you need to do to grow your sales and team. Negative attitudes will only ever hold you back.

So your mindset is of paramount importance and the recipe for success is correct mindset + consistent effort over a period of time = successful business.

**Call to Action**

- What's your mindset? Learn to change this if the way you think is holding you back

- Are you in a retail trap? If so, re-evaluate

- Focus on being consistent, instead of on results

- Get used to changing those hats!

**Notes**

"Our business is infested with idiots who try to impress by using pretentious jargon."

David Ogilvy

# Key 7

## Build for wealth, not title

Your company will have some sort of compensation, career path or commission structure illustrating where and *how* the money is made. It's a guide and a planning tool. All the various levels have different changes in status or title and in line with that there is usually a bonus or a increase in commission. You join the business to make money so it's only wise to understand what you need to achieve at the various different levels where the commission payouts get a little higher. However, all too often what can happen is you can get almost seduced by fancy titles or company incentives, such as cars and holidays. I remember feeling like this for sure. A title or incentive is a *recognition* of your achievement – it is a by-product of building your business *correctly.* You firstly need to establish *how much* you want to earn and *where* in the commission or compensation plan you need to be. It's not about achieving a certain title, it's about the most *efficient and stable way* of getting you to your income destination and what really matters is the money going into your bank account. Understand the ins and outs of the commission plan and structure your business for income. Plan your sponsoring or recruiting strategy and structure your business around your financial goals, not the title.  Grasp the first steps you need to take and what needs to be achieved – you don't want to be missing out on income through lack of understanding, which happened to me in my very first sales cycle - this is not good business  planning!

## Optimum vs Minimum

The commission plan will only show you the minimum requirements needed at that particular level. To get the most out of any commission plan, you need to *overachieve* at that level.  If you set out to do the bare minimum you require to achieve a certain position or commission level, then you are heading for trouble and create a 'spinning plates' scenario which is damned uncomfortable! Learn to work to optimums, not to minimums. Always overachieve at whatever level you are aiming for – you will then always be very profitable at that level and you'll never put yourself in the situation of worrying about whether you'll maintain your qualification every cycle. If you are unsure, go through the commission plan with your most credible upline – they will have a much better understanding of it and will be able to help you with setting your first few goals of where you want to achieve and how much you want to earn.  Commission plans vary from company to company and often they can be quite difficult to grasp so if you don't understand it *fully* at first, then keep on looking over it.  Many companies use jargon in some description. Find out what the jargon means – never be afraid to ask a question, ask, ask and ask again. There will usually be a central contact centre you can call who can provide you with answers for any jargon you may need clarifying, but for the best advice go to your upline for any questions on how the commission plan works as they are actively working the business.

## What's in a title?

Avoid getting too consumed by fancy titles. There will always be titles to aim for along with a shiny new badge to wear. Always bear in mind that you joined the business for income, for money, not for a badge or a title. Naturally the new title adds importance and makes you feel good and in some instances, gives you more kudos. However, I have seen situations in my career where someone is intent on getting the new title and may not necessarily build their business correctly and these people 'hide' behind new titles, not necessarily having created or maintained their business correctly to back up their title. I have also seen on many occasions where distributors get far too consumed with the kudos of having a certain title and may not even be 'maintaining' that title with the necessary sales volume, therefore they may not be earning what you *think* they are! Kudos does not pay the bills! It's the paper and metal that goes into the bank every month or every sales cycle that matters, nothing else! Please take it from me - always build your business for maximum profit and the title will come along the way with the money; aim to have more distributors and sales than is set out in the company compensation plan or commission structure; that way you'll always be building a team that is profitable.

## How can I sell the opportunity if I'm not earning 'big' money?

This is something I hear a lot and at the end of the day, all of the high earners within your company started off with nothing when they joined. I remember 'selling' my opportunity in the early days of my business when I was earning just a small amount of commission. It's the vision that you have for your business that will sell it. If you have unshakable vision yourself, this enthusiasm transfers itself. Attitudes are contagious – is yours worth catching?

> *" A man can succeed at almost anything for which he has unlimited enthusiasm."*
> Charles Schwab

If you are passionate and enthusiastic about something then others can feel that and you don't need to explain. Enthusiasm is transferred. Selling is all about a transfer of feeling, not convincing. If you doubt yourself and doubt if you'll ever get to the top of your company or indeed earn very good money, then people will reflect that back to you in the things they say to you – unfortunately life is a reflection of what you are thinking. Law of Attraction is always at work in every situation.

You will always have a credible upline that you can fall back on and use their success story to help you build your business if you feel you need that extra credibility. Use the testimonials, but always do the talking yourself if you can. Get your upline to help encourage your new prospect by talking to them on your behalf. Please do remember that *most* people don't join Direct Sales for large incomes – they join for an extra income and it is afterwards they see the bigger picture and what is available. So, don't get too hung up if you're new and feel that you're not equipped to 'sell' the bigger picture because you're not 'there' yet. You are the best advocate for your opportunity; after all, you're involved with it and have taken the time to learn more so you can create more – you're reading this book for starters! Pioneers in your company didn't have any stories, just sheer enthusiasm and vision that the business would grow and prosper for anyone involved.

## Call to Action

- Set a plan to build for maximum profit

- Overachieve at your current level

- Understand the plan thoroughly

- Focus on a strong stable business and forget the next title

### Notes

*"Think of business systems as bridges.*
*Bridges that will provide a path*
*for you to cross safely...*
*to financial freedom..."*

**Robert Kiyosaki**

# Key 8

## Follow a 'Success System'

Your company will have a business system in place to help propel you forward. In fact, all successful companies have business systems in place to ensure that the company is operating at its optimum level and processes can be repeated by more than one individual. The most famous of these that we all know is the McDonald's™ system. It's the McDonald's™ best practice guide that is absolutely non-negotiable; and that is why whichever country in the world you go in, you know *exactly* what you're going to get! From the timing of the fries to the construction of the burger, there is a simple system to follow, so simple that you'll often find 18-year-olds running the outlets! Every Big Mac™, whichever country in the world you go in, will taste and be constructed in the exact same way– now that's what you call an effective system! Obviously I'm talking about a very well-known franchise here and most franchising operates in the same way – you take a proven business idea, buy into it, and run it in the exact same way. Your Direct Selling business is like a mini franchise: as a Direct Seller, you are 'buying' into the company framework, (most Direct Selling companies require a small investment) agree to represent the company in accordance with their terms and conditions, and expand it with your own flair and initiative in return for commissions. There will be proven and effective ways of going about building your customers and team, and it's important to follow this, so find out what this system is.

*TOP TIP! Successful distributors and pioneers within your company have blazed a trail for you to follow. It's a simple task. Just follow it. Have the blind faith that if it's worked for others, it will work for you too.*

Certain leaders within the industry and within your company may have proven ways of building customers and teams and my advice is to follow the advice you're given by the person that recruits you. They will present to you a method of the *best way* you should go about certain things, which will be a success system; don't deviate from this, just follow it. That's exactly what a system is; it's something that when followed, works. This will be a tried and tested way of doing things that works in order for you to start building a customer base and your network of distributors. The usual recipe for any Direct Selling company is the same: retail (find customers) – recruit (new distributors) – teach your distributors to do the same (find customers and, if they wish, recruit new distributors). A simple system. However, for a system to work effectively, all parts of it must be in place. For instance, if you only find customers and never recruit, the system is failing and you'll find that you're not moving forward. If you recruit but never teach anyone else to recruit, then again the system has failed and you're not moving forward. If you recruit and never retail any product, you'll have a team that are going to follow you and not retail any product. It's like rowing a boat with one oar – you'll only ever go around in circles! Therefore, if there is the *best* way to sell the product, *follow that*. What is the average order of a customer? And how many customers do you need to turn a profit? Are there any better ways to retail the product? There will also be the best way of sponsoring or recruiting; how many leads do you need to be generating per week? What do you say to a prospect when they enquire about your business? What is the quickest way to sponsor/recruit? How many new recruits do you need immediately? How best to conduct the initial meeting with your new prospect? These questions, and many more, will all be part of a success system. From generating a lead, the optimum number of leads to generate, to following a set script, to getting your new distributor up and running, there will be a system to follow. And here's a clue: if it works for others, it will work for you too!

*"If you could find out what the most successful people did in any area and then you did the same thing over and over, you'd eventually get the same results they do."*
**Brian Tracy**

## Don't be a maverick!

Quite frequently I have witnessed new distributors question their upline when presented with a formula for success and do things their own way. When they don't get the results they want, guess what? It's usually the upline that gets the blame! If you find you're not following set systems, practices and examples on building your business, don't expect to get the best results. Please do listen carefully to the person who has introduced you when they are guiding you with the right thing to do. Whatever is recommended to you as the best way of building your business, simply follow the advice if you want to get the best results. Please don't try and reinvent the wheel.

 *"The definition of madness: doing the same thing over and over and expecting different results!"*

Many a time I have recruited new people into my team who just haven't listened to the advice that I have given them, for them only to come back to me and tell me that things aren't working out for them. It's then a case of, "I told you so..." It is advice, of course – you are an independent distributor and you do not have to follow whatever is recommended as the best way of doing this; the decision is yours. However, remember this important fact: your upline has a vested interest in your business. If you succeed, they succeed. Does your upline want you to fail? Of course not! Direct Sales is a business where if you help others succeed, you succeed. So your success is dependant upon how successful your team is. Your upline wouldn't advise or recommend that you do anything that is not going to be of benefit to you. Therefore, whatever advice or information they impart, just follow it. It stands to reason.

## Call to Action

- What is your success system? Find out

- Follow every aspect of your system to the letter - don't deviate

- Follow what your upline guides you need to do - don't second guess!

## Notes

"Nourish the mind
like you would your body.
The mind cannot survive
on junk food."

Jim Rohn

# Key 9

## Be an avid learner

To achieve significant heights in any career is going to take a fair amount of learning. Your Direct Sales business isn't any different; it's a new career and it's important that you treat it like that. I have learned so much in the last 16 years of being in Direct Sales, from reading books and listening to CD programmes, to attending training meetings and seminars. Today, I still keep learning. You can never stop learning. The room for personal development is never big enough – there's always room to grow. There is a plethora of information out there on Direct Sales and Network Marketing, and also self-help and personal development. You will be drawing upon lots of skills that you already possess and you are also going to expose many skills and attributes you need to develop, and that's not a bad thing. Identify your strengths and improve on your weaknesses. On a clean sheet of paper, draw a line down the centre and make a list of everything you're good at on one side and on the other a list of where you need to improve. It's the person you become that will eventually lead you to higher success.

> ## *"In order to earn an above average income, you need to focus upon becoming an above average person."*

So for instance, if you find that your time management needs some attention, then read a book on time management. If you're not that confident, get a book on boosting your confidence, such as *Feel the Fear and Do it Anyway* by Dr Susan Jeffers. If your interpersonal skills need improving, then get a book on building better relationships, such as *Personality Plus* by Dr Florence Littauer. And the list can go on. There's so much available online via Amazon and available to download on Kindle that information is really just the touch of a button away.

The moment you join a Direct Selling business, you're going to be presented with lots of new training and the first of this learning comes in the form of your business manual to learn about your company and the commission plan. It's important that you understand the commission plan, systems and processes, policies and procedures of your company. What is of the utmost of importance is your own personal and professional growth and development. Your upline may recommend books to read about your industry to aid your development as a Direct Selling professional. My advice is read whatever is recommended to you and what 'jumps out' to you. You may have heard this before: 'the more you learn, the more you earn' and 'leaders and readers and readers are leaders'. Sounds like a cliché in our industry but it's so true. Direct Selling is a professional industry and treat your business as professionally as you would a new career. Treat it like a hobby and it will pay you like hobby does; treat it seriously like a professional career move and it will eventually reward you financially. But remember, hobbies also cost you money.

*"As long as you're green, you're growing.*
*As soon as you're ripe, you start to rot."*
**Ray Kroc, founder of McDonald's**

## Importance of events

Incorporated into your Direct Selling business will be regular training sessions and opportunity meetings, seminars and conferences. Training sessions and opportunity meetings may be more frequent and are usually more intimate, smaller events whereas seminars and conferences tend to be larger events quarterly, bi-annually or annually. These are great to get along to for inspiration, motivation, somewhere to take your new prospects – why train them yourself when someone who is more experienced can! You'll gain new ideas, it will help reinforce your belief in your company, you'll meet new people, make new friends and, most importantly, you'll begin to gain more confidence in yourself to progress further. Rubbing shoulders with others who have the same focus will only ever be conducive to your success.

> *"Get around the right people.*
> *Associate with positive, goal-oriented people*
> *who encourage and inspire you."*
> **Brian Tracy**

You become the type of person that you associate with. Success breeds success. Whatever the frequency, my advice is to get along to any events you can; a small nugget of information could be priceless to you. Events act as a boost and can be the catalyst for you to stay inspired and motivated, especially if you're going through a few challenges which can happen from time to time. I'll guarantee you'll feel far better for attending than if you hadn't, especially if you did drag yourself kicking and screaming to one! The great aspect about Direct Selling is that you are in business for yourself, but you're *never by yourself.*

> **Here's something I once heard –**
> *"If you're not feeling so great, you need the meeting.*
> *If you're feeling on top of the world,*
> *the meeting needs you!"*

Everyone is bringing to the table at training meets and seminars with their presence, from the speakers and the hosts to the attendees – there are givers and takers in all situations in terms of people's presence; why do you think institutes like Weight Watchers™ work so well? Losing weight isn't difficult, but the meetings help people stay focused, plus the sharing, the inspiration and the 'togetherness' keeps people going. Therefore, getting along to a positive, uplifting environment where you can meet others and get some new training will always leave you feeling better about yourself once you've come away from it. I never stop learning and even now, I can attend a training meeting and can learn a brand new method of doing something which I can incorporate into my business from a brand new distributor. Having the humility to learn from anyone, no matter how new they are, is a great quality to possess.

**Call to Action**

- Do you attend events regularly?

- Write a list of your strengths and weaknesses and work on improving

- Make some influential friends within your social circle

**Notes**

"It takes twenty years to become
an overnight success."

**Eddie Cantor**

# Key 10

## No overnight successes!

There is no such thing or person who is an overnight success in Direct Sales. Residual income takes time and there are going to be challenges along the way, as with anything in life. Often, I have seen instances where newer distributors look at the successful people within their organisation or company and think, "Oh, it's alright for them, they're successful because they're a couple and building it together," or, "It's okay for her, she could build a big business because she has no children," or "It's alright for them. They got in at the start; that's why they're doing so well." This is really the wrong mentality to adopt and will hinder your success if you do find yourself thinking like this. The simple truth is that it's not okay for anyone who has become successful in Direct Sales. Everyone has had their own journey, and their own trials and tribulations to contend with. Everyone has their own mountain to climb so there is never an overnight sensation. You won't see the climb, you'll just see them when they're at the top reaping the rewards of their business. To begin to get to the levels where you start to create a good five-figure income from your Direct Sales business, you are looking at a four to five year plan and most people at the top of your company will have taken four to five years of graft and *consistent* effort to get there.

## Success is a journey

You've probably heard this phrase before: success is a journey, not a destination. It's the person you become along the way that will lead you to your eventual success and this is true for the people who are at the top in Direct Sales. Whichever company you have joined, you have the same starter kit, the same products, the same general public, the same training – so why do some get to the top and others do not? It's simple: belief and consistency. Here's a great excerpt from *The Treasury Of Quotes* by Jim Rohn to illustrate my point:

*Motivation is a mystery. Why does one salesperson see his first prospect at seven in the morning and another salesperson is just getting out of bed at eleven? I don't know. It's part of the mysteries of life.*

*Give a lecture to a thousand people. One walks out and says, "I'm going to change my life." Another walks out with a yawn, muttering to himself, "I've heard all of this before." Why is that? Why wouldn't both be affected the same way? Another mystery.*

*The millionaire says to a thousand people, "I read this book and it started me on the road to wealth." Guess how many go out and get the book? Very few. Isn't that incredible? Why wouldn't everyone get the book? A mystery of life.*

You have the same opportunity that everyone has within your business. For sure, your set of personal circumstances will be different from those of your peers. However, it's what you decide to choose to do, or choose not to do that will eventually lead to how successful you are.

## Conviction and belief

I've touched on this before: have total conviction and belief in what you're doing and in yourself. Total conviction and belief allows you to immerse yourself within what you're representing, work with full intention and this helps you to keep getting positive results. If there is any doubt in your mind at all, it is like a slow puncture; it will deflate your belief, and will stop you from doing the small things every day to lead you to eventual success. Total conviction allows you to act like the best, before you are the best. Total conviction allows you to act like the success you're going to become, before you get there. Total conviction is an attitude to adopt.

*"To guarantee success,*
*act as if it were impossible to fail."*
**Dorothea Brande**

Success is all about simple disciplines repeated every day. Failure is the opposite: a lack of judgement and failure to take action, repeated too often which accumulates to being off course to promises made to ourselves. Be sure to work your plan consistently over a course of time, to reap the positive rewards of cause and effect. If you're consistent and make the correct choices, choosing to make that extra prospecting call, choosing to attend that meeting that will help your thinking, working an extra evening rather than taking the night off – it's good choices that accumulate into long-term success. Conversely, if you slow down your efforts, if you don't read that book which will help your thinking, if you choose to take the night off rather than attend the training that may just have given you a winning idea to change the course of your business, the effect may be that you miss out on valuable opportunities to grow your business, hence delaying your future success. Success will just push itself that little bit further away from you.

## The power of ONE

This is how successful people become successful. They do more. They don't settle for being average or having average results. The power of ONE is powerful. Make ONE more call every day; attend ONE more meeting to learn; read ONE more book that will help change your thinking; find ONE more customer. Just when you think you have done enough, learn to push yourself that little bit further. The ONE more principle will accumulate over time, compound into more and more long-term success. Small things add up and it's the little things you do on a consistent basis that will add up to long-term success. Learn to adopt the mentality of doing a little bit more. Success is a state of mind that can be learned and practiced.

*"Success is a state of mind. If you want success,
start thinking of yourself as a success."*
**Joyce Brothers**

## Think like a pioneer

If others can build a successful business, you can too. Don't always wait for answers and to be told by your upline; be proactive and find answers, learn for yourself that's how any greatness is born. By using your initiative, you will learn far more and become a better and stronger leader. It's the responsibility of your upline to guide you, but you don't have to sit and wait to be guided. Just like pioneers, leaders don't wait. They make their own decisions, try new ideas and take responsibility for their future. Your end goal may seem a million miles away, but have vision.

*"Vision is the art of seeing things invisible."*
**Jonathan Swift**

Vision is what builds cities and vision will help you build your business. Use that vision to create goals. Be clear about your end result and then break your journey up into 'base camps'. Use the commission structure to help you plan where you want to be and by when, within certain time frames. Learning to plan your business, staying focused and consistent is what separates the successful from the average within this industry.

**Call to Action**

- Adopt the 'One More' principle - do one more thing every day

- Learn to be *consistently* consistent

- Make your five year plan for success

- Break your journey into 'base camps'

**Notes**

"It's not the hours you put in...
but what you put into the hours."

# Key 11

## Don't give up your day job

This Key is going to provide you with sound advice in a financial sense, so please pay attention!

Are you working your business around your job? You may initially join a Direct Sales company for the additional financial benefits to enhance your current lifestyle. It's normally the case that you see the potential and the bigger picture, once you become involved in your Direct Selling business, that you can create from it a full-time income. So, fairly quickly your focus can shift from earning an extra income to the possibility of making a full-time income and being able to give up your job. When you get along to training meetings and seminars as part of your company, you get exposed to the successful distributors who have created for themselves the magical PM/PT equation – Plenty Money/Plenty Time, living the dream life and enjoying the lifestyle which they have taken many years to get to and being able to 'retire' from the nine to five rat race. Upon first blush, you can look at these distributors and feel almost romanced with the idea of being full-time within your company; what you haven't seen are the years of sheer effort they have dedicated to get to their position. Over the years I have seen so many new distributors try and go 'full-time' with their Direct Selling business prematurely and consider themselves 'retired' from the rat race, but only then to find themselves struggling to make ends meet trying to build their Direct Selling business. Remember, being retired is about having an *independent income* regardless of your level of effort. Time + Money = FREEDOM. You can't have one without the other.

 *"Being retired is about income, not age. It's about not having to work and still having an income."*

You are running your business for *extra* money and my advice is simple: keep your day job and build another full-time income alongside your job. This is business savvy and will put you in a VERY strong position. If you are a couple, you can create a third 'wage' with your Direct Selling business– how powerful is that? If you are single, then you can double your disposable income and this then creates opportunities for you. Leaving your job prematurely can put you under unnecessary financial and undue pressure; most of us are not natural entrepreneurs who can thrive under this kind of pressure. I built my current business under massive financial pressure: I lost my full-time income overnight in January 2007 and found myself building my new Direct Sales business with no other income coming in, under huge financial pressure; I had every day bills to pay, I had a mountain of debt to deal with, my overdraft at its limit, borrowing money off my mother and not a lot of income being produced from my *brand new* Direct Sales business. My only saving grace was I had the focus and desire of where I needed to get to; I was passionate about the company and had total belief and conviction in myself and in the product; couple that with a good work ethic and I swiftly began to build a successful business. However, building a business when you have NO REGULAR INCOME to keep you afloat is not ideal circumstances and you have to think very carefully if you really would want to build a business under this kind of financial pressure.

## Part-time hours; full-time attitude

If you build your business part-time around your current job, then you create freedom from credit card debts, loans and mortgage burden. It gives you the freedom to invest, save and head towards financial freedom. For example, you can pay off your credit cards, offset or even pay off your mortgage. You can invest your Direct Sales income into other income streams - another property, investments - you are in *business*, so be wise and treat what you are doing *like* a business!

Here's my advice: only go full-time with your business once you have doubled your day salary with your Direct Sales business. Whatever you are earning in your weekly or monthly pay packet, aim to first match that income with your Direct Selling business and then go on to double this. This extra income can create your freedom.

Let's get down to brass tracks - you will need to invest back into your business within certain areas for it to grow. You may need to invest in various ways to promote and market yourself, your product and opportunity. You should be investing in your personal and professional development and with certain aspects of the running of your team. Most of the successful Direct Sellers I know have invested into their business in order for it to grow, therefore the salary you bring home from your day job will still be important to you. You will find it difficult to reinvest money if all you are earning is the money from your Direct Sales business. Unfortunately, I have seen it time and again when many distributors leave their jobs to 'focus' on their business, but it doesn't necessarily grow any quicker. Why? Because if you have a whole day to do something, you're going to take a whole day to do it! Here's a scenario: you have eight hours per day to run your business, you are trying to create more retail sales to compensate the fact that you need more income, you haven't got sufficient funds to reinvest in your business and you can spend time twiddling your thumbs in front of your computer, devising new plans and magical new leaflets that will miraculously bring you hundreds of enquiries and you spend more of your time checking emails, rather than getting out there recruiting new distributors, and think you are moving your business forward! Don't confuse accomplishment with activity.

Whatever activities you are engaging in, ask yourself, "Is what I'm doing *right now* making me money and moving me forward?" If the answer is no, then you need to change your plan of action. Unless you are finding new customers or talking to new people about your opportunity, or helping your current team members with growing their business, then you are not growing your business. Ensure that 90% of your time is spent with either new prospects and distributors.

 *"Get down to business, not busyness!"*

Stay in your job and put a full-time attitude into part-time hours. I agree, you will be sacrificing some of your leisure time but that is a small price to pay for long-term freedom: you can pay the price for success or you *will* pay the price for failure. Know how many hours you want to dedicate to your Direct Selling business and cram as much as you can into those hours. You will get more done, I can assure you.

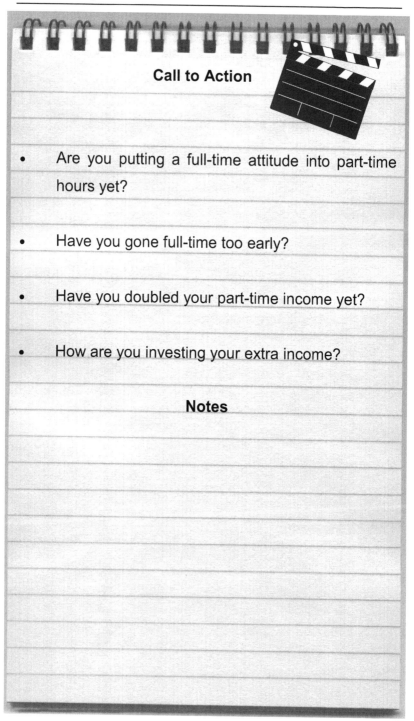

## Call to Action

- Are you putting a full-time attitude into part-time hours yet?

- Have you gone full-time too early?

- Have you doubled your part-time income yet?

- How are you investing your extra income?

## Notes

"There are no monuments erected for the critics in life."

# Key 12

## Never mind the 'naysayers'!

I think nearly every one of you reading will have encountered this at some point and if you haven't, then chances are you probably will at some point! That is encountering those members of the 'Moan and Groan Brigade' who make you feel dreadful every time you speak to them about your Direct Selling business. Unfortunately, not everyone is going to see the opportunities your Direct Sales business has to offer and often it's your nearest and dearest, such as your spouse, close family, friends and colleagues, who will be the culprits of trying to dissuade you from continuing to build your business. Some of these people will see the amount of effort you're dedicating in the early days, won't see your immediate financial gain and will proceed to tell you it's not worth doing, that it's a waste of time, that you're not earning enough money and to go and to get a 'proper' job! Have you heard some of this before? I'm sure you have – I certainly did and thank goodness I didn't listen to any of them. Simple philosophy to adopt here is: *don't take financial or business advice from people who are not involved in your business or industry.*

*"If you want to earn one hundred thousand per annum, don't take advice off people who are earning less than that."*

How can you listen to people who know nothing about your industry, your company or your products? Yet sometimes you feel you need to take on board their 'feedback' or comments which usually will be detrimental to your focus and progression! As much as we love our nearest and dearest, they can drain you of your passion and enthusiasm, if you allow them! So I feel it's important *not* to mix business with your personal life. Don't talk about it and don't share anything with these people; preserve your 'attitude' towards your business. That's what you have an upline for – they are equipped to give you advice and support about your business.

*"Ridicule has always been the enemy of enthusiasm, and the only worthy opponent to ridicule is success."*
**Oliver Goldsmith**

A sure-fire way to protect yourself is to have very clear and defined goals, a structured strategy and approach and therefore you will be very focused. The more focused you are, the more you'll learn to listen to yourself and there will be no room for someone else's negative opinion to sway you as you'll know *exactly* where you're headed. Nothing can get in the way of someone who has unshakable belief and is completely single-minded to an end goal. As Eleanor Roosevelt said, "No one can make you feel inferior without your consent." *You choose* what you decide to think and it's your choice whether you allow other's comments to affect you or not. Their comments and opinions can become your reality, only if you allow it to. It's a choice to feel good or bad about something, so stop and think next time someone close to you shares a negative opinion about your business. It's an *opinion*: everyone's got one and they all stink! We're all entitled to one but it doesn't *mean* anything, only the meaning and emphasis you give it or allow it. So just ask yourself, "Am I going to take this opinion on board and choose to feel bad about it, or focus on my goals for myself and continue to feel good about myself?"

I have found over the years that reading or listening to personal development material will help you with personal and professional growth and development you need to remain focused, and regular attendance to training sessions and seminars will also be a fantastic help to keep you feeling positive and enthusiastic. Surround yourself with positive and like-minded people whenever you can and have regular contact with people that uplift you too.

If you do find yourself feeling dissuaded by others around you, take stock of your goals and review your 'reason why' you're involved in Direct Selling, which I covered earlier on. Without a big enough reason 'why', the 'how to' then becomes difficult, therefore other's negative comments and opinions will have a detrimental effect on you and impact on your business. Once your purpose is absolutely clear, it will almost create a shield, a barrier, and wild horses won't be able to stop you.

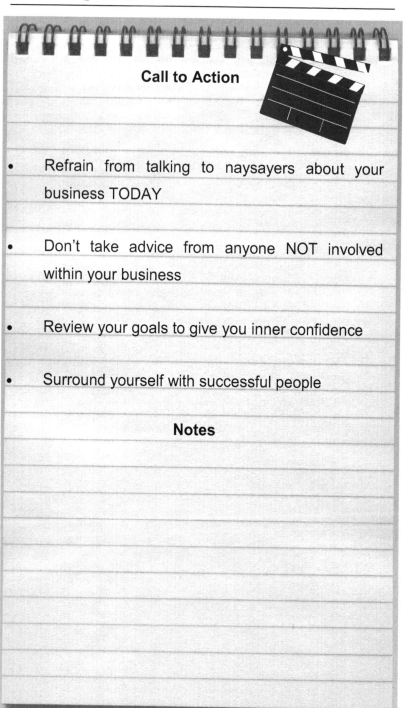

**Call to Action**

- Refrain from talking to naysayers about your business TODAY

- Don't take advice from anyone NOT involved within your business

- Review your goals to give you inner confidence

- Surround yourself with successful people

**Notes**

"People who want milk shouldn't sit on a stool in the middle of the field in hopes that a cow will back up to them."

# Key 13

## Lead generation

### Part I
### Talk to people you know

You may be thinking this is a little old school, in this digital age of social media where everything is viral in the palm of your hands with your smart phone or tablet or the click of a button away. However there is something very powerful about word of mouth, recommendation. Let's face it, word of mouth is the most powerful form of advertising. Think about if for one moment: what have you inadvertently advertised or recommended within the last few days? Within the last week? Or the last month? Perhaps it was a great restaurant. Or a fantastic movie. You recommended it. Did you get paid for it? No of course you didn't. We tell the people we know, our family and friends and share our best experiences with the people we know. It also makes perfect sense to share your new Direct Selling business with people you know and I'm going to share with you ideas on how to go about this so you feel confident about marketing your new business.

Although this book is called Direct Selling Success, you are simply marketing your Company, hence the term Network Marketing which many Direct Selling companies are. What is marketing? Getting a new idea, concept, product or service known. Therefore, you're more in the marketing of your business rather than the selling or convincing business. Let me get you to look at it this way: if you started any other business, let's say you've just started car valeting business, what's the very first thing you'd do? You read my mind. You'd tell everyone you know that you've just started a car valeting business (part of your marketing strategy) and if anyone needs a clean car, to come to you! You're not asking them to have their car cleaned there and then. You're letting everyone know you have a new service that can benefit them and not to go anywhere else. So why is it with your new direct selling business, you want to keep it to yourself and not market it to everyone you know?

Here's step one. Set your mindset correctly. If you don't know what you're involved in or what you've got in your hands, you're not going to be effective when approaching those you know. Therefore understand the commission plan and the awards plan and KNOW what you've got in your hands.

## Making a list

For a successful list, you must first write it down. DON'T KEEP IT IN YOUR HEAD. Have a permanent record book and keep it with you ALL THE TIME. If something great happens with your day and your business, and you want to share it with someone, you have your list to hand. So when the mood strikes you and you're feeling more motivated than usual, you can make that call. Another crucial point is to not prejudge. You generally tend to leave people off your list because:

1. You don't realise what you've got in your hands
   or
2. You have a misconception of how good people have got it

As human beings, we naturally tend to judge people by our own set of circumstances. For instance, a broke person with a dead end job won't put people on their contact list who are earning twice what they may be earning. What these people don't realise is that higher earners can be broke but just at a higher lifestyle – if you spend more than you make, it doesn't matter how much you make! However another point to stress about people that earn higher incomes is this: they have had a certain discipline to get that far. For instance, they may have had to study more and work harder and it also tells you that they are interested in achievement.

## How to sort and approach people on your list

People will join your direct selling business for different reasons. Who do you know who would like one or more of the following that your direct selling business can provide:

- Freedom – financial independence and escape from the rat race
- Self employment – with a conventional business, your business ends up running you! Not with Direct Sales and network marketing
- Security – jobs are not for life
- Retirement – it takes money, not age, to retire, so who do you know would like to retire early

Also, who do I know who:

- Wants to improve their life and add a good cashflow to it
- Would like to spend more time with family and children
- Wants to retire early
- Don't like their job
- Would like to be recognised more
- Wants to have their own business

These are the benefits that your Direct Selling business can provide, these are the benefits. People don't work for money, but for what money can do for them.

Also, here's another train of thought. Look for people who take the lead in life and take responsibility, for little or no financial gain. For example, head of your local neighbourhood watch, those who volunteer for social causes in their spare time, fundraisers and those who participate in events for charitable causes, parents who get involved with your child's school, the person that runs a local slimming group, who do you know is great at organising parties and a great host? These people aren't necessarily the most financially successful but they are people who take responsibility and who make things happen. Busy people usually do well at everything they do.

## Timing

Timing is crucial. Unfortunately, you won't know when the timing is right for someone, you just have to offer your opportunity to them. Generally, someone must be shown an opportunity when they are somewhat receptive, when something in their life is not quite right and they want to make a change, so their decision to join you does boil down to timing.

## Keep records

A percentage of people who turn you down may join you at some point if they see you continue with your Direct Selling business and become more successful. So learn to stay in touch with people – I like to call it drip feeding people information. A "No" rarely means no. It means:

- Timing is not right
- They don't know if they could become successful
- They are not convinced they could make it work
- They are afraid to start
- They have preconceived ideas about what you're offering

127

If someone says No to you, the worst thing you can do is keep pestering them. Learn to step back, carry on regardless and let them see that you're doing it anyway. As you become more successful and get results, some of them may eventually join.

## Your approach

You can use the third party approach to talk to people you know which is a great way to spike interest in someone. Often, trying an indirect way can get a person's attention, something like this:

"Hey Debbie, I know you're pretty involved with your teaching job at the moment and I know you haven't got any time; I'm just looking for five key people to help expand my business; the right kind of people are earning around £25,000 within a couple of years and it doesn't interfere at all with what they're doing. Could you give me the names of one or two people you know who might be inclined to look at something like that?"

Debbie may say, "Well what's that all about then – I'd have a look."

You say, "Well, I really wasn't even thinking of you Debbie. You're really busy with what you do and I really didn't think you had the time, but I'll show you and you can see what you think".

The third party approach really works to get the other person to look at your business!

## Don't talk too much!

I know how it feels to be new in this industry –you've got an amazing product, there are some fantastic incentives, you can win cars and holidays and some of the top earners are millionaires! And you want to tell the whole world how fantastic this new business is and how everyone you know needs to be involved and they'd be crazy not to!! Take a breath for a second. Enthusiasm is great. But trying to tell people far too much will repel them and without realising you can come across too aggressive. There is a danger of saying far too much, people will think you're crazy and won't join you!

Look at this scenario: you're going to feed hungry birds in the park and taking a packet of their favourite seeds and bread crumbs. What would happen if you ran into the park, really enthusiastic, waving your hands and said, "hey, birds, I've got loads of your favourite seeds to eat!!!" No matter how hungry the birds are, what are they going to do? Of course, fly away! However, if you were sat quietly on a bench, just throwing your seeds and breadcrumbs, before you know it you'll be surrounded by a huge flock of birds. So when prospecting and approaching other people about your business, be gentle and listen to others, gather information: who has had a new baby and wants to stay at home, who is unhappy in their job, who needs a holiday but can't afford to or who do you know who wants to refurbish their home but cannot afford to do so. These are just examples of problems people have, and you can offer the solution.

## Remember F.O.R.M

When you're building your list of prospects, you can learn to talk to people wherever you go and create more prospects for your business and add names to your contact list. Learn to build a rapport with people you may see quite often: the checkout girl, the petrol station cashier, the person who serves you at the bank. Rather than jumping in there (like the birds in the park) learn to cultivate rapport by using F.O.R.M. – Family, Occupation, Recreation, Money. People tend to talk about these subjects and thereby you'll get to know someone's circumstances and when you feel the timing is right, you can show them your opportunity. They will be much more willing to listen and warm to you, just like the birds in the park.

## Lead Generation
## Part II

## Generating prospects

Wouldn't it be great if prospects lined up outside your front door all the way down the street to join your business every day! If only it worked like that, we'd all be millionaires pretty quickly! However, it doesn't and the life blood of building your team is to generate prospects. Prospect leads are the fuel for your business; just as a driving instructor needs fuel for his car to run his business, the fuel for your Direct Selling business is leads. Without leads, you are never going to grow a team. Before you begin to generate leads, it's a good idea to understand the commission plan so you know how to structure your team and so you know where you're headed. Have a clear idea of how many people you need to reach your first level and then double it. As I've mentioned before, always overachieve at any level at which you are aiming, before aiming for the next level, and never ever work on minimums. If your commission plan stipulates a certain number of distributors or a specific amount of sales to be produced at a particular level in the commission plan, you need to at least double the requirement, so ensure you are safely achieving your level. Therefore, it is important to continually generate as many leads as you possibly can using different, tried and tested methods and of course there's always new methods; nothing is exhaustive. No one way is better than another. If you are *not* generating enquiries for your opportunity, you are going to stand still.

*"Be not afraid of going slowly,*
*be afraid only of standing still."*
**Chinese Proverb**

## Some 'How To's'

Here's some important advice and that is never to use your personal home telephone or personal mobile/cell phone to market yourself. Use a secondary handset – eBay is great to find a low cost secondary mobile/cell phone handset. Record a dedicated voicemail so any callers know they have reached the correct number and whenever this phone rings, you *know it*'s for business. It stands to reason to separate your personal life from your business life. Once you start to earn more, you may want to invest in free phone/toll free number or a non-geographic number which gives you a more national feel and may encourage people to call from beyond your locality. Work local, think global.

With regards to your web presence, some Direct Selling companies will provide a sub-domain facility for you to use whilst other companies allow you to build your own site. Ensure your website URL is also on all of your offline literature – there are many prospects still to be found offline. Set up a Facebook business page and try and keep your Facebook page name the same or similar to that which you have chosen for your website. This helps with your own personal branding and keeps you looking consistent whether someone lands on your website or finds you on Facebook. Offline strategies also work. Gain advice from your upline if you wish to place advertisements online or in local printed media, such as newspapers, and find out the best types of wording that will attract more attention.

Also, your upline should provide you with a basic script of what to say over the phone once you call the person back which you can adapt once you get accustomed to speaking to strangers over the phone. Your method of dealing with the leads may differ depending upon the company that you work with; you may email information or a video prior to calling the prospect. Or you may just call the prospect straight away with information on your opportunity. Either way, it doesn't matter what method you use to contact the prospect enquiring. What is important is using a wide variety of methods to generate leads.

 *TOP TIP! Deal with enquiries the same day they come in and if you can't, at least within 24 hours.*

Leads can go 'cold' if you don't deal with them immediately.

## Ideas to generate leads

Here's a list of different ways of generating leads that I've used to build my business and they all work:

- One-to-one prospecting door to door
- Google Adwords
- Business to business
- Town centres prospecting
- Careers fayres
- Shopping centres
- Business magazines
- Social media (Facebook, Twitter, LinkedIn etc)
- Online directory sites
- Talk to anyone you meet and hand out cards
- Online forums and discussions
- Join local clubs within your area
- Gym
- Customers
- Referrals
- Newspapers
- Networking groups

- Leaflets through doors
- Postcards in shop windows
- Car adverts
- Yellow Pages – contact local business owners
- Phone book
- School gates
- Summer fayres
- Cross selling
- Calling 'Jobs Wanted' adverts
- Mailing lists
- Telesales callers and door-to-door callers – talk to these people rather than tell them you're not interested

No one way is better than another and over the years I've recruited people into my business from *all* of those different methods. You don't know where you're going to recruit your next team member from. Therefore, your job is simply to utilise as many techniques as you can to get your marketing material with your contact details out there in the marketplace. It goes without saying that the more you get your marketing material out there, the more likely you are to find more and more new prospects. Consider these methods as 'fishing rods' and your 'pond' being the marketplace – the more 'fishing rods' you have out there, the more likely you are to get enquiries, conversely the less rods you have then it lessens the chances of getting enquiries. Your aim is to be generating fresh enquiries every week and not being too reliant on the team you have already. A key here is to always sponsor or recruit on a replacement basis, i.e. replace the last person you recruited.

## Avoid 'management' mode

I've seen distributors do this and I have been guilty of it myself when you slip into 'management' mode: this is a situation where you've got a few distributors in your team and you want to 'look after' them before you sponsor or recruit anyone else which really is just resting on your laurels and a euphemism for laziness. You can easily look after the ones you have and also find more new distributors at the same time. Avoid falling into this trap as you will stall momentum within your business. Remember what I talked about previously – the power of ONE to keep your business going in the right direction. You also can become a little 'stale' if you're not actively working your business and therefore you can get out of touch with your business fairly quickly.

*"There are world leaders; have you ever heard of world 'managers'?"*

## Prospecting tips

Wear your business 'hat' wherever you go.  You don't know who you are going to meet or talk to at any particular point that may benefit from your business.  Life is throwing you opportunity in the form of chance meetings all the time and it's up to you whether you choose to take them. You can have telesales calls at home, retail staff in high street stores, door-to-door sellers, supermarket checkout staff, and the list can carry one.  These are people that you may not necessarily see or speak to ever again so take the chance meeting as an opportunity to speak to them. Staying focused helps you to create and spot opportunities. What is the worst thing that can happen? Someone will say "No" to you. I've mentioned before that a "Yes" and a "No" go hand in hand in Direct Sales. However, letting the rejection affect you is public enemy No.1 for Direct Sellers and carrying negative feelings and a bad attitude can allow you to miss opportunities and therefore miss out on potential leads. Refrain from carrying negative feelings from one "No" to another person. Treat every lead you generate with the individuality they deserve.

## Tips on approaching people

Remember F.O.R.M. that I spoke about before? Family, Occupation, Recreation and Money; using these lifestyle points as a conversation starter is a great way to illustrate your opportunity. Some good tips when approaching people directly on a face-to-face basis is to offer something: a product sample, a brochure, for example. When you 'give' something away, the prospect may be more inclined to give you their name and number. After all, merely handing out marketing material and not getting any follow up details is pretty much futile and consider it a dead lead. You've left the ball entirely in their court for them to contact you, if they decide to do so. So, whenever you prospect on a face-to-face basis, the minimum you should get is a first name and contact number. Often, even when someone is interested in what you've got to offer, they won't call you. The fortune is *always* in the follow up. Therefore, contact prospects within 24 hours whilst the conversation is still fresh in their mind, which I refer to as a 'hot' lead; leads can go 'cold' if you don't follow up swiftly.

If the person is not interested at a particular time, always keep their details in a file or on a database that you can revisit at a later date. As I've mentioned before, you don't necessarily go looking for a business, it can often find you and when the timing is right for them, people will join you. I have spoken to prospects on many occasions where they had been approached by someone before but the timing had not been right but they kept the idea on the back burner. They then responded to an advertisement of mine as the original person had not maintained contact with them. My point is keep *all* of your leads and revisit them. If the timing is not right for someone, ask them when would be a better time to speak to them about the opportunity, make a note in your diary and contact them again.

## Plan your action

*"He who every morning plans the*
*transactions of the day,*
*and follows out the plan,*
*carries a thread that will guide him*
*through the labyrinth of the most busy life.*
*But where no plan is laid,*
*chaos will soon reign."*
**Victor Hugo**

Failing to plan is planning to fail. Have a plan each week of *how* you want to generate your leads, day by day, and

137

then set out to work your plan. Avoid haphazardly floating through your week; I can assure you, you won't get anything done. Have weekly planners, 'to do' lists and a plan of action you can monitor. It will help immensely with your time management. Plan your week in 'real time'. Have a daily planner that starts when you rise and ends when you sleep and plan in various methods you are going to use that week to market your business. This will help you to learn to focus on activity, not results. Being too overly results oriented can be counterproductive to you if you continually focus on how much effort you're inputting in comparison to the amount of leads generated. The two are never going to tally and if you're not careful it can leave you feeling demoralised! How many times have you seen an advertisement for a particular product over and over again and not paid any attention to it? However, when you're in need of that product, the advert practically jumps out at you even though you've seen it what seems like a million times before! The same rule applies to your business – what someone ignored a year ago may be quite pertinent to them now so you just have to keep on getting your marketing information out there. You have to be quite mechanical and robotic about it. Just keep on doing the tasks that you need to do to get your business building. Repetition is the mother of skill *and* success.

**Call to Action**

- Mix up your marketing methods

- Learn to wear your 'hat' all the time

- Plan your diary in real time

- Revisit all your leads if the timing is not right

**Notes**

"Investing is laying out money today
to receive more money tomorrow."
**Warren Buffet**

# Key 14

## Invest in your business

I do hope you found some great ideas in Key 13 on marketing your business. It's all about generating as much interest as possible in your business, product or service. There will be a necessity to reinvest back into your business. If your business relies on product demonstration, then you'll need to invest in products. In order to build your team, you will at times need to reinvest a portion of what you earn into advertising, although there is a lot of free lead generation online and offline that you can do. Let me pre-empt a common misconception. You may be thinking, "Well I've started my Direct Selling business to *make* money, not *spend* money." Well, yes, that is true. However, when you're reinvesting in your business, you're not *spending,* there is a difference between reinvesting and spending. Spending money has no future reward; it just gives instant gratification depending on whether or not you've spent it on yourself or not! Reinvesting is for a future gain or reward. My advice to anyone is to look at what you want from your business before you decide how much you are going to invest. Why are you involved?

Remember the three types of people that join Direct Selling? Where do you fit into this, and which one are you? The answer to that question will determine how much you want to invest in your business, if at all anything.

## Why have you joined?

The level you invest in your business is dependant upon why you've joined and where you fit into it. Remember the three types of people that get involved. If, for you, it's just about earning a little bit extra to enhance your lifestyle and you're happy building your business at a slower pace, then you may just need a few simple marketing materials and engage in no cost or low cost online and offline strategies. If you are a seriously looking at your Direct Selling business for the long-term and a serious income, then look at your strategy. If your goal is to build a massive organisation, then incorporate into your strategy gaining as many leads as you possibly can and work as hard as you possibly can to gain some momentum within your business. Therefore, this may involve a degree of reinvesting back into your business early on. I recall my very early days with my Direct Selling business and making calculated decisions to reinvest into my business. This was *far* from an easy decision to make when I had a mountain of debt to contend with at the time and couldn't afford it. But I couldn't afford not to. It was a *calculated* decision; I couldn't afford financially at the time but understood the value of speculating.

When you are investing in your business, you are actually investing in *you* and your future. I sometimes hear distributors saying, "I've joined to make money, I don't want to spend it!" I don't know of any successful person in Direct Selling who has a massive organisation and hasn't done it without investing some of their own profits back into it. Accept that if you want to grow a *large* business *long-term* which will create you a residual income, then you are going to have to invest into it to make it grow some more. You've heard of the saying speculate to accumulate and that's exactly what you're doing.

**Call to Action**

- What do you want from your business?

- How quickly do you want your business to grow, and how much do you want to invest?

- Have you got a strategy of what advertising you need to invest in?

**Notes**

"Time is our most valuable asset,
yet we tend to waste it, kill it,
and spend it, rather than invest it."
Jim Rohn

# Key 15

## Time management

L et me begin with this:

### TIME

Imagine there is a bank that credits your account each morning with 86,000 pence. It carries no balance over form day to day.

Every evening, it deletes whatever balance you failed to use during the day.

What would you do? Draw out every penny. of course!

We all have such a bank – it is called TIME.

Every morning, we are credited with 86,400 seconds. Every night, it writes off as lost whatever you haven't used. It carries over no balance and allows no overdraft.

Every day opens a new account for you, each night it burns the remains of the day. If you fail to use the day's deposit, it is your loss.

There is no going back. There is no drawing against tomorrow. You must live in the present, on today's deposits. Invest it so you get from it the utmost in health, happiness and success.

The clock is running. Make the most of today.

To realise the value of one year, ask a student who failed a grade.

To realise the value of one minute, ask a person who has just missed a train.

To realise the value of one millisecond, ask someone who won silver at the Olympics.

To realise the value of a lifetime, ask someone who wasted it and did nothing with it.

Treasure every moment you have and treasure it more because you shared it with someone special – special enough to spend your time with.

And remember – time waits for no one.

Yesterday is history. Tomorrow is a mystery. Today is a gift; that's why they call it present.

I think time management is about one thing: prioritising. It's never been one of my strongest points, which I've had to work on (and I continue to work on). Many of you reading will be running your Direct Sales business around other jobs, spouses and children, so good time management to get the most out of your business **is of the essence.**

## Keep a diary

If you don't already keep a diary, then start one today! Whether it's on your smartphone, tablet or a good old fashioned diary, learn to make lists and write things down. Here's a really good saying I once heard: "Feeling listless? Then make a list!" Put everything in your diary and write a list for everything you need to do. I keep everything in the one diary so I don't double book, personal and business engagements, to avoid getting into a mess. As soon as a thought or idea comes into my mind, I make a note on my smartphone or diary, whatever I have at hand. Don't trust your memory!

## Plan once a week

Never start your week until it's finished on paper. What do I mean by that? Well, on a Sunday evening, sit down and put five minutes aside to plan when you're free to run your business. Never haphazardly begin your working week without a clue of what you want to achieve. If you don't know where you're headed, then how are you ever going to get there? I find weekly planners are excellent. Have a planner that you can actually pin up on your fridge or office wall, shade out all the times that you're unavailable to work your business; visual aids are great. You'll then be able to see the blocks and pockets of time you have available and plan what you are going to put into those hours.

## Prioritise

Once you can see where your free time is, whatever you put into those hours needs to be prioritised into business building activities; inert activities can be done after hours. Prioritise things such as prospecting, lead generation, contacting team members and producing personal sales. Further down the list should be paperwork, and checking and sending emails, which can be done first thing in the morning or in the evening. Also plan in any training sessions that you may want to attend. Your week needs to be completely structured – it's up to you how and when you work, but without daily and weekly focus you will find that you'll be drifting along aimlessly and you won't necessarily achieve anything. Avoid focusing on monthly tasks; you cannot focus that far ahead. Plan week-by-week and then break that down into daily tasks. It's far easier to focus on daily tasks and checking them off as you accomplish, rather than focusing on the week or month ahead. However, it is important to know what you want to have achieved by the end of the month which you will have broken down into daily tasks which are manageable. If you don't write things down and focus, then you'll inevitably look back and be saying to yourself, "Where on earth have the last few months gone? My business still hasn't grown!"

Break down your week by asking yourself a few questions and planning around them, such as:

- What is my aim?
- How many sales do I want to produce?
- How many new recruits do I want?
- How am I going to find them?

Tick things off as they are completed on your 'to do' list as this will give you a sense of achievement.

## Procrastinate later!

If you don't like doing something, but it is necessary that you HAVE to do it, put it towards the beginning of your list. Get it out the way first so then you'll look forward to the rest of your day or week. I've learned this from running. I organise my route to get all the uphill runs done at the start of my run, so it's then downhill all the way home. If there are activities which are optional that you don't enjoy doing to grow your business, then don't plan it into your week – you just won't do it and you will begin to approach your business reluctantly.  Do the things that you LIKE doing – it's your business so enjoy every minute of it!

## Time stealers!

When you're working from home, you'll have distractions, time stealers – TV, lengthy phone calls, washing, ironing, the mother wanting you to take her shopping! When you've planned in work for your business, that's all you should be doing in those hours. Employ yourself! When you're doing something you know you shouldn't be within your work hours for your business, ask yourself, "Would I want to employ me right now?" If the answer is NO, then change what you're doing immediately! Your work hours are there for *work*. You are your *own boss* so go to work for *YOU*. Don't let yourself down with distractions – only you will have a sense of guilt later.

*"When you do the things you ought to do,*
*when you ought to do them,*
*the day will come when you will be able to do the things*
*you want to do,*
*when you want to do them."*
**Zig Ziglar**

**Call to Action**

- Turn your monthly goals into daily plans

- If you don't like doing it, don't plan it into your week

- Learn to prioritise business building tasks

- Avoid time stealers

**Notes**

*"Goals are the fuel in the furnace of achievement."*

**Brian Tracy**

# Key 16

## Goal setting

I f you don't know where you're going, you're never going to get there. And once you have decided where you're going, you'll require the 'drive' to complete your journey. As you're aware by now, building a long lasting income and business is going to involve a little bit of hard work and determination. Therefore, you need a big enough reason *why* you are joining and *why* you want to continue with it to keep pulling you through; it will make all the 'how to' training simple to action and it will help you through the challenges and stay focused. You have ups and downs in everyday life and in your day job, and Direct Selling is no different. However, you haven't got a boss to show up for or be answerable to every day so you need to be answerable to yourself. You need to 'show up' for yourself every day. So it's important to have something that is going to drive you. What is your reason for joining? What is your driving factor that will keep you going through the ups and downs? Your upline is there to guide you, inspire you and motivate you, but you cannot rely on that. You may have been shown some success stories to inspire you as you embark on your journey. However, it's your own goals that are going to drive you and give you the internal nudge from within to keep going and take action. It will become one of the key building blocks of your success; if you can think something, you can achieve it.

## Two types of goals: personal and business

What has worked for me is having clear and separate personal and business goals. It's your work efforts that will lead you to getting what you want personally. We don't just work for money but what money can do for us, otherwise it's just paper and metal in our purse or wallet! I believe what you want personally can really drive how hard we work and give a strong enough reason to get out of bed in the morning. Therefore, it's the inspiration that comes from your personal goals which will lead you to fulfil your business goals. Both go very much hand-in-hand. The two are interlinked and drive one another. You have to think long and hard about this. We're all made up differently and what makes one person tick may bore the living daylights out of another! Start with your personal goals – they have to be strong enough to want to get you out of bed. They may include:

- Dream holiday
- Things for your children or spouse
- Possessions you'd like – e.g. new car
- Getting out of your job
- Your home – improving or moving
- Being your own boss

- Saving more
- Affording more luxuries

And goals don't have to be material things:

- The type of person you want to become
- A personal ambition you'd like to fulfil
- A person you'd like to impress
- Someone's life you want to change

And here are some more thought provoking questions:

- What do I want?
- Where do I want to go?
- What do I want to see?
- What do I want to have?
- Who do I want to be?

 *"Until you commit your goals to paper you have intentions that are seeds without soil."*

You've got to have a, "What am I willing to work hard for?" list. Have some easy things to reach on your goals list and some not so easy things. For instance, you may want to treat yourselves to a meal out at an expensive new restaurant which has opened in your area. This may be a little closer than getting your dream home. Do you see my point? Have short and longer-term goals. Looking too long-term means you won't have the sense of urgency to work NOW – looking too short-term will not give you the aim of what you want to achieve in the bigger picture of your life. So be clear and be sure to have short-term goals that you'd like to achieve as well as long-term goals. As you achieve short-term goals, you get a sense of achievement. If all of your goals are long-term, it can be demotivating as they are too far away from reach.

Your personal goals will give you the focus to set your business goals. You can place a monetary and time value on your business goals and then set out to achieve them. The commission plan is there for you to help you plan, which I think is a great tool in all Direct Selling companies. You also have your upline to help you. Here are some guidelines of what you may want to include in your business goals:

- How much you'd like to be earning (of course)
- How much sales volume you need
- How many people you need in your team
- Which 'level' in your commission plan is optimum
- How many leaders you need
- An annual turnover figure you'd like to attain

Be realistic with your goals: it's better to underestimate and overachieve, than to overestimate and underachieve. But they do need to stretch you. Your time management plan, which I covered in Key 15, will help you determine how many hours you have per week to devote to your business and in turn this will determine how quickly you achieve your business goals.

With both your personal and your business goals, never put limits on your success. Think big!

## Goals: the 'how to'

Goals need to be **S.M.A.R.T** – **S**pecific, **M**easurable, **A**ttainable, **R**ealistic, **T**ime Specific

**Example of a SMART personal goal:**
I will have saved £1,000 by 12th August 2012 as spending money for my holiday to Cyprus on 30th September 2012.

**Example of non SMART personal goal:**
I want to save more money in the next six months for my holiday in September.

**Example of a SMART business goal:**
By 31st December 2012, I want to have 100 distributors in my team, with monthly sales of £50,000 and an income of £2,000 per month.

**Example of a non SMART business goal:**
By the end of the year, I want to be earning more money and have a much bigger team.

Can you see the difference? The first statement makes you feel more clear and focused; the second statement a little fuzzy and hazy. The fact is that you're not going to achieve the second statements in either examples, but I hear so many distributors in this industry talk this way. The more clear and defined you are, the more likely you are to achieve what you want.

## 'How to's' on your personal goals

I suggest you take some time out each day and think about your goals until you have a definite list that *really* fires you up – don't sit down in one afternoon and cram planning your life out! After all, do you plan your holiday in a few hours? No! You look around, browse, take the time off, if you're like me you plan what you're going to wear, plan your itinerary, and every detail; you don't just do this in a few hours, you can take weeks! So, please give your life as much attention as you would do a holiday – learn to give yourself the time, the rest of your life is so much more important than one holiday. Have an itinerary for your life! Give each one a time scale to measure your achievements; if it's something quite small, give it a few months, if it's something bigger, perhaps a year or two. Have fun with this! Get a Vision Board – images are powerful and words are powerful – they have to excite you. So be childlike and get the images of the lifestyle you're aiming for as a reminder of why you are working and put this board in a prominent place. This is your 'reason why' in one place staring at you every day and your daily reminder for what you are working for. Take your time to plan your goals. Something else to think about: which decade are you in? How many decades have you got left? On our epitaph, we will all have a dash – what will yours say? You really want to live your dash.

*"There'll be two dates on your tombstone*
*and all your friends will read 'em.*
*But all that's gonna matter*
*is that little dash between 'em."*
**Kevin Welch**

## 'How to's on your business goals

The great thing about Direct Selling is the fantastic commission structure we have which really helps to make plans and goals. All companies have some definition of a sales cycle that we work towards, which is a fantastic aid in breaking goals down into manageable chunks. Before you begin, start with the end in mind. Know where you want your business to be at the end of the year and then plan backwards, month-by-month, sales cycle after sales cycle. Include in your goals numbers of new distributors you want, income you want to generate, sales volume you want, levels in the commission structure that you want to reach. Put all of these projections on a spreadsheet. As you then begin to go about your business, you can then fill your spreadsheet out, month-by-month, and see if you're on or off track. It doesn't matter if you're off track – on track or off track, you need to see where you're headed. This way you can readjust your goals accordingly, and make them bigger or smaller.

## A mistake to avoid...

A big mistake many distributors make is putting their 'team' into their goals. **Learn to put your people around your plans, NOT your plans around your people.** Not sure what I mean? The plan comes first; the people afterward. For example, let's say you have Sally, Bob and Cynthia in your team, and when revisiting your goals, you could be thinking, "Well, Sally will become my next Super Leader, and Bob will become my Senior Leader, and Cynthia will be my Starlight Leader, which will make me a Double Diamond Deluxe Leader!" In reality, this is great. You have no idea what may happen in the lives of Sally, Bob and Cynthia and they may not come through for you – so your plan could fall apart. Learn to set your goals and work towards them, *no matter* who is in your team. Just *have faith* and belief that you'll get there. As Martin Luther King once said, "Take the first step in faith. You don't have to see the whole staircase, just the first step." The dynamics of your team can change overnight; all you need to do is stay focused in the direction of where you are headed, learn not to focus in the moment of what is happening at any particular point. A journey keeps progressing forward and your business is a journey. If you always focus in the moment of what you have at that particular point, the 'what if's, and doubt begins to creep in. An aeroplane on its journey is off course for most of the flight. If the pilot focused in the moment on all the times he is off course, we'd never get anywhere! Declare what you want and keep going in that direction - failure should not be an option.

## You can move the goal post

Another important point to remember is that goals can always be adjusted. If you're working harder and exceeding your goals, change them, set them higher to stretch yourself and achieve more. If you're a little off track, then move the goal post back a little. Learning to monitor yourself part and parcel goes back to the Measurable in SMART goals. Does it mean you've failed if you haven't got exactly what you want? Not at all. Success is failure turned inside out. I can guarantee you'll be far more advanced in your business having set your goals than not having set them. As the saying goes, "Shoot for the moon. Even if you miss, you'll land among the stars." The only way to fail is by not having any goals. Small steps are better than staying still.

## Fear of failure

You may not have set goals previously for fear of failure. Commonly you won't set a goal if you don't truly believe you can reach it and because it doesn't excite you. Here is a famous quote:

> *"Glory lies in the attempt to reach one's goal*
> *and not in reaching it."*
> **Mahatma Gandhi**

You will learn far more from the negatives in life than the positives – so if you aim for something and don't get it, or it doesn't go quite right for you, then you've learnt something along the way. You'll never learn from positives. So with regards to your goals, declare them; this means you are then committed to them. Too many people are fearful of what others will think if you miss your goal. One thing to take on board here is this: it's not the score card that someone else keeps on your life that counts; it's the score card that you keep on your life that makes the difference.

## Fear of success

This is almost like the fear of the unknown. Some of you may fear setting big goals because of the worry of 'coping' with a larger team and worrying about how you will manage in a new role with possibly bigger responsibilities. Whether you feel ready or not, begin the journey; don't keep waiting for the *right* time or perfect conditions. If you do, you'll never get anything done and you'll never really get started. Embrace the unknown and embrace change. Once you learn to embrace change, you will become more and more confident. Often when you throw yourself into a situation, whether or not you feel ready to do so, you will quickly adapt and you will grow and learn quickly. The human mind is amazing in how quickly we can adapt to new circumstances and stretch our own abilities.

**Call to Action**

- Split your goals into personal and business goals

- Work your plan regardless of who is in your team

- Revise your vision board - if it excites you, then it is a true goal

- Don't wait for the right time, just DO IT!

**Notes**

"If you want 1 year of prosperity,
grow grain.
If you want 10 years of prosperity,
grow trees.
If you want 100 years of prosperity,
grow people."
**Chinese Proverb**

# Key 17

## Running your team

irect Selling is a people business and you will learn how to bring the best out of your team. I've learned over the years through trial and error and may have lost the odd distributor along the way through ignorance or lack of understanding. You need tact, common sense and understand that when you're motivating your team, you have to take yourself out of the equation completely! I could dedicate a whole book on team leading, leadership and people skills as this subject is by far one of the most important things you need to learn in this industry. Essentially Direct Selling is a people business. However, what I have done is given you some important nuggets on what I feel will help you initially with your team.

### Bite-sized chunks

Overloading a new distributor with months and years of information is something I have been guilty of! Only 7% of what you actually say is heard; 35% is tone of voice and

58% is body language. You've heard the phrase, "How do you eat an elephant?" So when you're eyeball to eyeball with your brand new distributor, the key thing for them is: getting them out there and finding customers, therefore making money. That, I feel, is the number one fundamental MOST important factor when seeing your new distributor for the first time – everything else is superfluous. On the first meeting, you need to establish their motivations, how much they're looking to earn and how to fulfil that immediately so getting your new distributor confident with selling the product or service is the most important thing you can do. Remember the three types of people that join this industry that I mentioned in Key 1 – where does your new distributor fit in?

Don't feel inclined to tell them all the intricacies of the commission plan, the incentives that your company lay on and how many top earners there are as *most* people do not initially join to earn thousands. I say *most* people don't. If you encounter that third type of person looking to build a large business, and they ask questions, then yes, tell them what is available immediately. Ensure your new distributor has a basic understanding and feel confident so that when you leave them initially they are happy to start selling the product or service and finding new customers. At the end of the day, this is *what* they are going to be teaching to the prospects they sponsor or recruit. The initial meeting should last no more than one hour. If it does, then you are definitely going into the information overload terrain! Set another meeting with your new distributor the same day that you have your initial introduction with them and ensure you both have the date in your diary; you'll be able to cover more training on a second meeting and this also helps begin to build a rapport with them. Training can be conducted remotely and facilities such as Skype are a tremendous resource for this.

Other training information pertinent to your company can be drip-fed over the course of their first few weeks. This will also give you different reasons to be contacting them too. If they ask a question and are ahead of your training schedule, then answer it. Some of your distributors will be more interactive with you than others and you will learn to crawl with crawlers, walk with the walkers and run with the runners.

 *TOP TIP! If someone is very interactive with you and asking lots of questions, this is a sure-fire sign that they want to move forward with their business QUICKLY.*

## Business Killer

Don't ever talk about anything negative that might happen to your new distributor; cross that bridge *if* they come to it! Unfortunate things that happened to you may *never* happen to your new distributor so you don't want to put them off before they've begun. Let me give you a scenario. What would a surgeon say to you before an operation? He's going to say that he's going to perform a procedure and when you awake from the anaesthetic, you'll be a little sore but you'll be feeling so much better!

He's not going to go into the graphic detail of cutting you open with a scalpel, then being stitched up again, how much pain you're going to be in and how uncomfortable you may feel for weeks! Pretty grim analogy, I agree! My point is: don't talk about horrors that may not necessarily happen!

## Identifying the stars

How do you identify the stars in your business, the future leaders?  Here's a list of key points.

Personal Attributes:

*   Positive attitude – easy to talk to and a joy to be around
*   Uses initiative – will problem solve without you
*   Enterprising with their business – thinks of new ideas
*   Building a good customer base
*   Never complains
*   Asks questions – will contact you regularly
*   Takes responsibility for their actions
*   People person
*   Work ethic – not afraid to work hard
*   Honest

Background: (not essential but can help)

*   has worked in Direct Sales before
*   professional career background
*   has run a business before

In my own experience, these are the factors that constitute good leaders within Direct Sales. Some will promote themselves straight away, others may need a little more persistence. If you find some are reluctant, don't try and push them into team building; if you identify someone and they're not quite ready, tell them you see potential in them but don't push someone along – you'll be in danger of losing them. People need to go at their own pace. Plant the seed and the "shoes will fit when the feet are big enough". Don't force people to go in a direction that you want them to go in. They will only quit.

## Contact

There are lots of ways to contact your new distributors: phone calls, video calls, email, text, social media, such as Facebook and Twitter. However, nothing beats a good old fashioned phone call but in these busy times any contact is good. When you have a new person in your team, contact them at least twice per week for the first two weeks so you can build a rapport with them, and it will give them the confidence to begin contacting you, which is where you want to get them to as quickly as possible. It's easier for 100 distributors to contact you than for you to contact 100 distributors. However, establish that once a level of competency has been achieved, that it's important for them to contact you.

Monthly e-newsletters are a great way of contacting your distributors, passing on important information, recognising new achievements, giving out training tips and ideas and allows feedback from your distributors. This doesn't need to be elaborate; just learn to set up distribution lists on email. Try and put as much information on the email rather than on attachments; this way it's easier to pick up the information via smartphones which is the way forward with mobile technology. They need to appeal to everyone in your team so be sure to include figures, facts, pictures, recognition, good news stories, company updates and important dates to keep your newsletters fresh, current and interesting. This then keeps all personality types happy!

Facebook is a great way of keeping in contact. When adding distributors on Facebook, put them in a separate group or list, or set up a separate account altogether – it's important to separate your business from your personal affairs. At the end of the day, your team don't need to know what you had for dinner and what you were up to on a Saturday night! Stick to business and just promote the products or service, talk about events, recognition and training tips.

## Recognition and reward

We all love to be recognised and the feeling it gives us for our hard work! Recognition is key to your business growth and it is a well-known fact that people work harder for recognition than they do for money. Everyone wants to feel appreciated and valued for their time and effort. Everyone wants to feel special and important. Always be finding ways of encouraging your team through praise and recognising their efforts. There is a key point here: you can only praise or recognise a *particular effort* a person has put in. So, let me reiterate: you're recognising the *effort* that the person has done or something they have *achieved*, not the person. Recognise them in several ways: individually, so send them a congratulatory card or message to tell them they've done well, and recognise publicly via your newsletters or Facebook – this also helps set the bar for others in the team and creates healthy competition. People LOVE to see their name in print and will work harder in order to maintain the recognition for another month. Your company may have a recognition programme and automatically send out certificates and pins. However, I've always felt that it's good to have your own programme in place too that is specific to you and your team, such as sending out your own certificates and rewards.

## Crawlers, walkers and runners

Often you want more for your distributors than they want for themselves from their business. When they progress, naturally you progress. The key to good leadership is learning to understand your distributors and give them the guidance best suited to *their level* of drive and commitment. You cannot deal with people with a 'one size fits all' attitude and approach. It's not rocket  science either learning to understanding how to guide  others effectively and go at their pace.  Mentally you can divide your team members into three – crawlers, walkers and runners. You'll determine who fits into which category simply from the first few conversations and meetings with them *and* by their actions:

what they **do** rather than what they **tell** you they're going to do. In fact, it goes back to the three types of people that get involved in Direct Sales: part-time income seekers, full-time income seekers and serious business builders. Someone's actions are usually the best indicator for you to ascertain their level of commitment, how much you need to guide and encourage them, and how responsive they will be towards your suggestions of how they can forge forward with their business. Of course, some people can talk a good talk but you soon find out who they are once a bit of pressure is applied and they bail out on you! You determine how much you can encourage and drive someone to higher levels by the amount of contact you get from them, phone calls, emails, questions – their 'wanting' to learn *combined* with appropriate action. If all you get is contact but they never seem to sell much or have anyone new to sponsor or recruit, you know they are a talker and you can step back a little. On the other hand, if you sponsor or recruit someone who wants to 'see how it goes' for a few months, but then produces fantastic results in retail and the team building, then you know they're possibly a runner in the making, therefore you can step in and offer your support and steer them onto a winning formula. What you shouldn't do is 'push' people into doing more than they want to do for your benefit, OR hold people back who are trying to forge forward (which is usually a reflection of an inert leader). In both situations, you'll end up with frustrated distributors and this can cause them to quit.

## Be the solution finder

You are the crux of your business and from time to time your team are going to encounter a few hurdles, which inevitably you may have been through too. Good leaders are solution finders, which you have to learn to become. When faced with an issue or a problem, listen to what is being said, agree and *empathise* (don't sympathise; there is a big difference between the two) and then offer your feedback and a solution to the problem. If they continue to moan and complain that something has gone wrong or not according to plan, then address the issue that you're there to help them find a solution to their problem. Don't ever feel inclined to 'jump in the pit' with them and start to put all the wrongs to right; if you do this then you are setting yourself and your new distributor up for failure. They will then view you as a sounding board, not as a leader, and you will continually get negative, draining phone calls from them of how bad things are for them, and it will do *nothing* for your morale or theirs. Start as you mean to go on. You have to be pro-active and offer your hand of support and pull them out of the situation. Nothing in life in perfect and nothing or no one is infallible. Good leaders are pragmatic; get some background information on the situation if you can – go on a fact find if needs be before addressing the issue, which is what I often do before speaking with the person in question and coming up with a solution. Remember you're not a social worker; find solutions to problems and if someone cannot accept your solution, then move on! As the saying goes, you can lead a horse to water, but you can't make it drink.

## Training and Events

Training can be done face-to-face or remotely, at arm's length. You should be trying to get new ideas and training out to your team regularly – weekly, monthly – the frequency is up to you, depending upon how your sales cycle operates, and the method of how you deliver is also your choice, depending upon how far and wide your team are. Keep up-to-date with any new information that your company has launched. Your team may not have kept up-to-date with new information releases so feed this out to them again. Face-to-face may not always logistically be possible so arm's length training in the form of emails, video conferencing or conference phone calls is a great idea of training. Group training is effective for generic information that applies to all. You may need one-to-one training that is pertinent to a particular person if they need specific guidance. Only spend one-to-one time with people if they warrant it. Please refer to my list of the attributes I've listed in Identifying your Stars. Your time is precious and time is also money – it's our main commodity in Direct Selling and needs to be invested wisely. If you feel a distributor is letting you down in any area then be happy to train them at arm's length.

Events can range from a small get-together in your home to hotel training meetings to large company-run events, but aim to get your team members along to any events if you possibly can. If you want to start with something in your home, it's simple and it's also duplicable. Anything is effective and it's all part of the contact. Events are an integral part of your business and it's the 'gel' for your team and helps with synergy and team spirit. It gets your team members inspired, motivated, feeling more refreshed, gaining new ideas, getting publicly recognised and meeting other team members. Often, you may have been trying to communicate a certain idea to one of your team members for months and it's reiterated at a training event, then the penny may finally drop if they hear someone else relaying the same information!

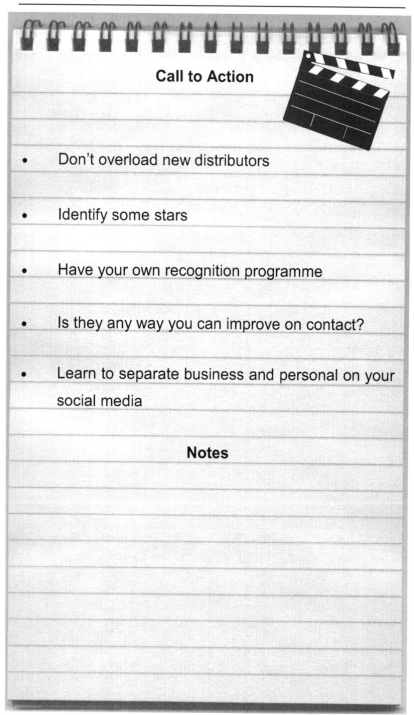

**Call to Action**

- Don't overload new distributors

- Identify some stars

- Have your own recognition programme

- Is they any way you can improve on contact?

- Learn to separate business and personal on your social media

**Notes**

"You can make money
or you can make excuses,
but you can't make both!"

# Key 18

## Excus-itis!

There are reasons why someone is successful, but usually excuses as to why they're not! Your Direct Selling business starts and stops with you. When you decide to join, you have made a promise to yourself and given yourself, with some guidance, the responsibility to make it grow. Excuses are like opinions – everyone's got one and they stink! Not taking accountability *will* hold you back. A mature attitude is learning to take full responsibility for where you are at any point with your business. It is very easy to pass blame; one of the most common things I hear is this: "If I had a better upline, I'd get better support and I'd have a bigger and better business!" It's the responsibility of your upline to provide you with the information, guidance and leadership you need to build your business. However, if you have an upline that may not be equipped with the knowledge for whatever reason, or is not the leader you would have wanted them to be, you have the power to go out and find out everything you need to build your business. In our digital age, information is at the tips of our fingers or just a phone call away. If your upline doesn't have the answer, someone out there will. With or without your upline, you have all the information at your fingertips to build your business. If you ask questions, you will find.

> *"Continuous learning is the key to the 21st Century, the information age."*
> **Robert Kiyosaki, author of *Rich Dad, Poor Dad***

## Take full responsibility

So long as you are making excuses or falling foul to blame for your lack of success, you will remain exactly where you are. If you have made a promise to yourself to do something in relation to your business and perhaps you've prioritised something else or procrastinated, be adult enough to assume responsibility for your lack of action. Stop right away with the old, "Oh but..." syndrome: "Oh but if only I'd have got in at the start. I'd be successful." "Oh but if I was running the business with a partner, it would grow quicker." "Oh but it's alright for her, she hasn't got children." There are many that I've heard over the years. Successful Direct Sellers don't make excuses. They accept where they are and their unique set of circumstances and get on with the task in hand. You can blame anything and everyone as to why you're not making your business grow or what is stopping you from achieving what you want to achieve. But whilst you are busy making excuses, someone else in your company with a fresh attitude will soar past you whose situation may be far worse but they have just embraced where they are at. I can appreciate we all have a work/life balance but I think procrastination is the *biggest* of time stealers. Getting into the 'blame game' will also stop you in your tracks: blaming your company, your customers, the product, your team, your upline, and the list goes on. If you don't like your company, find another one. If you don't like your product, find something you like. If you don't like the people in your team, then change the people. If you don't like your upline, go it alone! You don't need an upline to build a business. That's often why the pioneers of any business are great successes because they have no one else to follow, just themselves, using their own initiative and problem solving along the way, and the falling on the stumbling blocks of trial and error, only to get up and keep going again and again and again. A pioneer attitude and mentality is what a leader is, and this is the best mentality to adopt. I have learned FAR more using my own initiative than waiting to be told. Taking full responsibility for wherever you are in life, in my opinion, is one the highest degrees of personal development and it's the only way you can move forward from wherever you are. Staying in the mind frame of blame and excuses will inevitably hold you back.

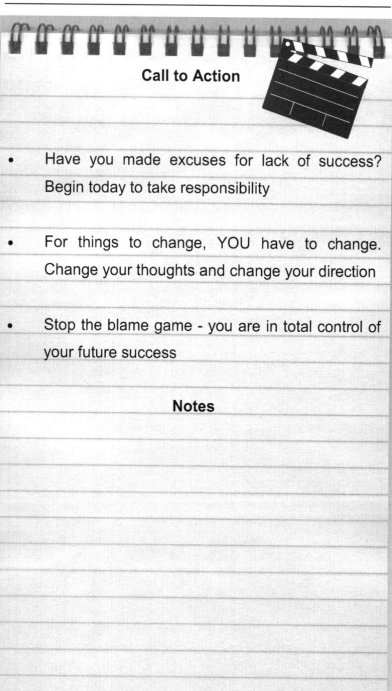

**Call to Action**

- Have you made excuses for lack of success? Begin today to take responsibility

- For things to change, YOU have to change. Change your thoughts and change your direction

- Stop the blame game - you are in total control of your future success

**Notes**

"If you focus on results,
you will never change.
If you focus on change,
you will get results."
**Jack Dixon**

# Key 19

## Focus on action, not results!

I f you opened a shop tomorrow, do you know how much you're going to sell, how many customers are going to walk through the door and how much you're going to turnover that week? You can do promotions, offers and incentives and advertise your new shop, but you can never predict the result. You're going to have slow days and you're going to have some bumper days in business, and your effort throughout will remain the same. You will show up every day at 7 a.m. and open your shop. At 7 p.m. every day, you'll close your shop. Day in and day out, six days per week, perhaps seven days if needs must. But you'll ALWAYS show up to open your business. No two days are ever going to be the same. Here's a question for you: if you have a slow day, will you close your shop halfway through the day and keep it closed the next day or for the rest of the week? Of course not! However, I have found that many Direct Sellers can have a bad day, or a slow week, and then almost stop and give up for the rest of that week or month. When you start a Direct Selling business, it's like opening a shop – you don't know how many sales you'll make or customers you'll find, you don't know how many people will join your team, you just have to keep applying yourself.

## Keep your 'shop' open

What many distributors do in this industry is compare the hours they have dedicated with the results they have produced and then slow down on their efforts to build their business, which is almost like closing your shop! By closing your 'shop', will your business grow any more or any quicker? This is fatal. You're not going to make more money by slowing down.

 *"Even if you're on the right track,*
*you'll get run over if you just sit there."*
**Will Rodgers**

There is never going to be a direct correlation between your effort and your end result, or your effort and your income. In regular jobs, we are conditioned to think in this way, that our time has an hourly rate or that a certain effort *has* to produce a result. Being too overly results oriented can really grind you down and it's counterproductive to think like this. Ask yourself this question: do you obsess about results? If so, begin to create the mindset to be action oriented and just stay focused on keeping your shop 'open' no matter who is going to walk into that shop or how much you're going to sell. Any type of business has no certainty on a daily or weekly basis; the only certainty is that with *consistent effort of self-promotion* you'll begin to create momentum hence the results will come through over a course of time. It's cumulative effort, or compound effort, little by little, day by day, that eventually builds up into long-term success. This is how successful people think in any walk of life; they keep the blinkers on and they just keep doing what needs to be done *regardless* of the results. They don't doubt, they don't second guess. Whereas on the other hand, the unsuccessful stop to look around them all time, at themselves and others, comparing the results against their efforts, and if results don't reflect their effort, they slow down. This in turn stalls any momentum they have created and then find themselves back at square one again wondering why their business isn't growing! As I mentioned previously, it's all about changing your mentality from 'employee mindset' to 'entrepreneur mindset'. Try not to expect too much from little or sporadic effort; it's about learning to keep your 'shop' open all times regardless of how many customers or new distributors you've found that week.

## Call to Action

- Promote yourself relentlessly every day

- Monitor the action of your daily tasks and disregard results

- Learn to keep your shop 'open', no matter what

## Notes

"In order for success to happen
you have to expect it first."
Yogeeta Mistry

# Key 20

## Expect success

This has been my motto for several years. I'd like all of you reading to understand that success lies within you. It's totally within you how far you progress within life. Your attitude ultimately will dictate your altitude in Direct Selling. There are so many sayings: "conceive, believe, achieve." "You are what you think." "Think and grow rich." "Whether you think you can or cannot, then you are right." However you perceive yourself and your business is going to affect how you get started and how you begin to progress with it. If you set out with a head full of doubt and an almost 'I'll poke it with a stick and see if it works' attitude, then you are off to a bad start. You have to have that knowing feeling, before you begin to achieve the success that you require, that it's going to happen for you. What do I mean by that? A knowing feeling is that feeling of expectation of having something before you get it.

## Winning the lottery

Imagine it's Saturday night and you're checking your Lotto numbers. As the announcer calls out the numbers, one by one, you realise that all six numbers are called out that you have printed on your ticket! How will you be feeling? Ecstatic would be an understatement! Even though the millions you've won are not physically in your bank account, you know you've won. That's what I mean by expecting to have something before you have it. Expect it. Have faith. You have to believe you're the best even when you're new to this industry before you become the best. You have to act like you're successful before you become a huge success. Act like a significant business person, because that's what you are. Intend whatever you want.

*"Take the first step in faith.*
*You don't have to see the whole staircase,*
*just take the first step."*
**Dr Martin Luther King**

You have to have that knowing feeling that it's going to work for you, hence it is so important that you choose your company wisely and have a firm belief in your product which will give you pride in what you're doing, and this pride alone will give you the confidence and enthusiasm you need. Your first source of inspiration should be from the people that surround you. Learn to surround yourself with positive and enthusiastic people within your company, including your upline. There is far too much negative in our society and far too much that people complain about: the government, the economy, debt, the rich get richer, the poor get poorer. Stop the negatives from encroaching into your life and learn to focus on things positively and generate good feelings from that.

Personal development is a major key to help you achieve the correct mindset. To begin with to keep you in the correct mindset every day, just list down three things every day that you are grateful for. Have a 'What I am grateful for' list. Be happy where you are before you draw what you want towards you. Continually complaining and focusing on what you haven't got will give you more of what you haven't got.

## What turned my life around

Personal development, for me, was the defining thing that changed the course of my life – I *always* had that knowing feeling that I would succeed with the *right* company. This came from learning about the Law of Attraction. This has played a MASSIVE part in my success and it is something that each and every one of you can and should learn how to harness and learn to understand it. I first learnt about the Law of Attraction in 2005 in the form if a DVD which many of you will have seen called *The Secret* and it changed my outlook and the course of my life forever. I was amazed! I began to read and learn more about this powerful law which I had no idea existed, and it was one of the major turning points for me. I attracted the company that I am involved with into my life, it has attracted the success that I desired, the leaders I needed and it continues to be a stream that keeps flowing if and so long as you allow it. How do you *feel* about the company that you are involved with? Law of Attraction responds to how you feel about things whether that is a good or a bad feeling; if you think you've joined a Direct Selling business and you feel so bad about it that it's not going to work for you, it won't! Law of Attraction responds to expectation; if you expect that you're going to progress with it, you will! If you expect it to be hard, it will be; if you have joined your company and have a problem with accepting a certain aspect of it, you are expecting it's going to be a struggle for you, and therefore it will be. If you expect that finding leaders is difficult, you won't. So feeling good about what you are doing is going to play a BIG part in your success. *Expect* to attract more leaders, *expect* to have a certain amount of sales, *expect* you're going to earn a specific amount of money – don't doubt and don't second guess – this is what holds most people back. You are your own worst enemy! Your mentality towards what you are doing is the key to your ultimate success.

If you doubt, you're hindering the right things from coming toward you and you will miss valuable opportunities to grow and expand your business simply because you won't be receptive to them. Negative feelings like anger, complaining and blaming will also hinder your success. You will attract into your life and business the way you predominantly feel. For things to change on the outside, you need to look inward first. For things to change, you must change.

There is a saying - become the type of person you want to meet. Therefore, if you want to attract more serious business-minded individuals, *become* that person. Become the person who doesn't gossip, who has drive, determination, who makes things happen and goes the extra mile. If you become this person, you'll attract those people into your business. The change has to occur within you before you see the change in your business. If you see yourself as someone who is just running their business part-time for a bit of extra cash, you're not going to be on the wavelength of the person who wants to make a serious change. Anyone can draw a line in the sand and start again. If you're unhappy with any aspect of your business, tomorrow is a new day and tomorrow can be a new you; the decision is yours. The harder you work on yourself and bring yourself higher, the more positive scenarios you'll attract into your life and business.

## Call to Action

- Success is a mindset: begin today to expect success

- Do you feel good about what you're doing?

- What do you think is difficult? Begin to change your perception on that aspect and begin to feel it's easy

- Make a 'What I am grateful for' list

## Notes

"Do not follow where the path may lead.
Go instead where there is no path
and leave a trail."
Harold R McAlindon

# Key 21

## Leadership and developing leaders

Leadership skills are something I've learned and honed and it can only be learned 'on the job', so to speak. You can read as much as you can about the topic and get all the theory in the world, but unless you are leading people, you are not going to get the experience. Leadership is fun and you'll meet a lot of wonderful people. It also has its challenges and I feel it's important to understand how to compose yourself as a leader in certain circumstances. Firstly, do not confuse yourself as a manager. Managers, as the term suggests, manage. They are often placed into that role and it is a title; a leader is a role model, a coach, someone that blazes a trail for others to follow. A leader will not always tell you what you want to hear but will be there to catch you when you are falling. As soon as you sponsor or recruit your first distributor, assume leadership; you have a responsibility to that individual. You'll also be finding other leaders within your business and it's important to learn to allow them as much autonomy as you can. Leaders make their own decisions, they don't look to others necessarily for permission or recognition, leaders don't gossip and rarely do they cause any trouble. They are just single minded and focused in one direction.

## Finding leaders

You need to be very lucky indeed if you think you're going to find your leaders all within your first year. Leaders are like eagles – you find them one by one. So it's very important to be realistic with your expectations. Natural leaders are rare, most leaders are developed. It's consistent recruiting and working the numbers which will eventually lead you to finding leaders and natural leaders too. The harder you work, the luckier you'll get so the more people you recruit, the more likely you are to find them. Don't become too 'desperate' to find your leaders too; I have met many distributors who become far too 'needy' and *desperately* want to find another leader to secure higher levels on the commission plan. A needy and desperate attitude will repel people from you. Your desperation will come over when you're talking to people over the phone or in person. The better approach is a more relaxed approach - you know what you need to do on your journey to Direct Selling Success which is to continue to sponsor or recruit new distributors with the expectation that, through the law of averages, leaders will come your way; often you'll find more than one at the same time. This goes back to Key 20, having expectation. If you doubt you're going to find leaders, then the fact is you won't, as that is your expectation. Questioning yourself continually is not creating the correct mindset. Life rewards you for hard work - often you get nothing at all or everything at once.

How do you spot a natural leader? Well quite easily: they have a sound understanding of what they want to achieve straight away. They will often keep you on the first meeting for hours and will ask every question under the sun. Contrary to most, they do not want to be drip-fed information and would prefer information overload. They will want to run with it straight away so be prepared for a sprint! Make sure you understand the commission plan fully as natural leaders will want to understand it from the start so they can plan on fulfilling their income needs. However, please don't feel that you can leave them to it; they still need hands-on guidance. The other type of leader are those who see the opportunity but have a slight reluctance in their own ability. Have many one-to-one sessions with these types of leaders, don't be inclined to cram too much information their way and beware of information overload. You need to structure their learning – place initial emphasis on all the hands-on aspects first such as telephone scripts and one-to-one recruiting, how to do a presentation, and being able to present the starter kit so they get the essential know-how of getting others involved. Next should be understanding the commission structure, helping them with effective goal setting and getting your new Distributor used to using company specific online applications which they will 'learn whilst they earn'. Coaching and teaching comes in stages so you need to approach different subjects accordingly with your new leader as and when situations arise. With any type of leader that comes into your business, be ready to help them plan ahead, they will need the hands-on guidance from you; leaders will have the vision and it's your job to take that vision and turn it into daily, tangible practicalities.

## Your role as a leader

You should be setting an example for your team and doing everything you're promoting and suggesting to your team. Leadership is not: do as I say, it's do as I do. Leadership is being at the forefront of your business, inspiring, motivating, trying new ideas, passing new ideas forward. Leaders know the way, go the way and show the way. It's the only way you keep your ear to the ground. You're not there to do it for anyone, to build someone's business for them. Show them, but don't hand-hold. This only leads to dependency and weak leaders.

## You can't avoid mistakes

Your team and your leaders are going to make mistakes from time to time. If you're a parent, you can't stop your child from falling over and the same applies to your new leader; you can't always be there all of the time and they will make mistakes but sometimes this can be the *best* teacher. No matter how much you guide someone, they are going to make mistakes. Leadership is a journey that is both rewarding and challenging. The one piece of advice I can give is that you cannot please everyone all of the time and don't try to, otherwise you will go crazy! Being a good leader means dealing with all kinds of people and situations. Just be the best you can be. Spend more time with those in your team who take responsibility for their actions, who don't gossip or play games and who are a joy to be around. Try and detach yourself from those who moan, gossip and complain and those who constantly want to point the finger of blame. The first sort of person is like a radiator – you'll want to be around them; the other is like a drain. You only have a certain amount of mental energy to expend and if you spend too much time trying to keep the 'drains' in your team happy, you'll have no energy for those who really need you.

## Negative and downline

Learn never to pass anything negative downline to your team. You may have frustrations from time to time and your team are going to go through the same. If you're having a bad day, or something hasn't quite gone to plan, then speak to your upline. Whatever you do, DON'T share your frustrations with your team! Negativity will KILL your business! How do you differentiate whether something is negative or not? Well did it make you feel good, or did it make you feel bad? Don't confide in your team with negative personal or business issues, no matter how you're feeling and no matter how mature you feel they are. If it made you feel bad, it will make someone else feel negative for certain. Whatever your team members go through, you may have been in that situation yourself so always be the solution finder for them and with any negatives you have, speak to your upline. Be the pillar of strength for your team at all times.

## Blame game

Unfortunately, some people may point the finger at anything but themselves for the lack of their success. Sometimes they may even point the finger at you. Everyone is self-employed in Direct Sales. You get your distributors started and show them the system. So long as you know you've been there for them and you've been the best 'you' that you can be, then your job is done. You've given your professional advice but if someone chooses not to take it or takes their eye off the ball, then it's not your fault. There are usually reasons why people are successful and excuses why they aren't. Learn to take responsibility for your own successes and failures, and this shift in attitude will help you mature into a good leader in this industry far quicker than those who finger point. If you find that someone is blaming their lack of success on you, or trying to 'hold you to ransom' that it's your fault that they missed a bonus, or the 'you owe me' scenario because 'you earn money off me therefore you're indispensable' attitude, then just listen and hold your composure and detach yourself mentally from it. You don't need to confront anyone; let them save face and just simply pull back and focus your attention on the more positive people in your team. Anyone can be successful *if they want to*. You don't need an upline to be successful.

## Dealing with conflict

Not an easy one. Try and stay away from it. It's easy to lose the battle and win the war, as they say! Good leadership is learning to judge a situation and knowing when to step back. If you find someone difficult to deal with, let them be difficult but don't lock horns with them; it won't pay. If someone is in a power struggle with you, let them have the power – they are in your team after all and letting the situation go will diffuse it, which is what you want. Whether they are right or you are right, what does it matter? If you're in the wrong, always admit it and take responsibility for any of your actions. If you feel that someone has an issue with you, then deal with the issue head-on. Refrain from sending emails or texts – they can easily be misconstrued. Simply pick up the phone and talk to them, ask the questions, mediate and get the problem solved, don't let it fester. Bring things tactfully to the surface.

## Dealing with gossip

> *"Don't be distracted by criticism.*
> *Remember – the only taste of success*
> *some people have is when they*
> *take a bite out of you."*
> **Zig Ziglar**

Sometimes in order for others to feel better about themselves, they feel the need to gossip. These are negative emotions that *will* hold you back. Success in any field can lead to others feeling jealous and resentful and the way these people cope with their emotions is to gossip. This happens as part of daily life and I think it's a part of human nature to want to talk about other people. Personally, I have learnt to stay within my bubble – you don't know when gossip is going to catch up with you! It can be hurtful but learn not take anything personally. Everyone has an opinion and we live in a free society. This is easier said than done but come from a position of understanding. People who gossip usually are lacking something in their life or are trying to justify their own lack of success. Be too busy with your own business to engage in such small talk. You will only be holding your success back if you do gossip.

## Personal vs business

*"Leaders must be close enough to relate to others, but far enough ahead to motivate them."*
**John C Maxwell**

Try not to cross the line of personal and business. Yes, you will be working closely with people in your team and relationships can be built quite quickly when you meet like-minded people, and some of them can become friends, but there is a fine line between leadership and friendship. If you need a confidante to talk to, talk to your upline and, if they are personal problems, your family and friends! Avoid getting too involved with your team members and their problems and personal situations. You are not a social worker, you are a leader helping someone with their business. Conversely, your team do not need to know every shred of your personal life either. Think about the corporate world: how much do you really know about the personal life of your Chairman/MD/CEO of your firm if you are employed, or have been at some stage? Learn to maintain a degree of respect with the people within your organisation.

**Call to Action**

- Never pass negative downline

- Be the pillar of strength for your team

- Try not to get too 'personal' with your team

- You can't shield your team from making their own mistakes

**Notes**

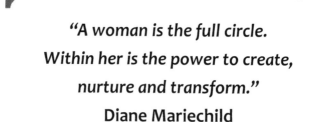

"A woman is the full circle.
Within her is the power to create,
nurture and transform."
Diane Mariechild

# Bonus Key 22

## Women in Direct Sales

L adies AND gentlemen, this Key is for ALL of you! As a single woman in this industry building the business by myself, I thought I'd like to include something from *my perspective* that can help you all, *especially* the women in business out there reading. For the guys out there, please don't skip this Key! This is not intended to isolate any of you and I do feel it's important for you to read this as it will help you learn to understand and communicate more effectively with the women within your teams. This Key has been taken from years of training men and women, making my own observations and learning the best way to effectively deal with people, often by my own trial and error. Some of you may agree with what I say, some of you may disagree but that's the beauty of the free world we live in and the choices we have.

What I've found over the years is because of what Direct Selling has to offer, a part-time home-based business, the industry does attract many women. On my quest to learn about the industry and become a better leader, a lot of the material I've read about our industry has been written by men and there were a lot of men at the top of the first company I ever joined. As a young woman coming into the industry, I found this difficult to relate to; I wanted female role models to follow, and there may be many women out there thinking and feeling the same. As I've matured into a strong leader in my own right, this fact has become less significant to me. Sure enough there are plenty of us out there making it big but sometimes I feel we don't just shout loud enough!

Women make fantastic Direct Sellers and there are many women in this industry making it big and building large and successful organisations. Women are naturally fantastic networkers. We are natural teachers and possess the innate ability to nurture, lead, organise and multitask which are all important business building skills. These innate abilities can be developed to use those life skills we possess into building powerful teams.

## From one woman to another

I certainly don't speak for all women here, but over the years, I have found that many women I've met, whom I found to be intelligent, competent and astute, do not recognise the qualities they have within them to progress, due to a lack of self-esteem and confidence. In my own experiences, this is brought about by coming out of a career to raise a family, divorce and becoming a single parent, feeling held back or unappreciated within their career or personal life, or making the wrong career choices. It could be a multitude or combination of things. You may be a stay-at-home mum building your business and yet you don't perceive yourself as the business woman you really are.  Many of these women I have met are intelligent and have attributes and skills they don't realise they possess UNTIL it takes someone else to point it out to them.  Some of these wonderful women are in my current team today who I am very proud of.  So from one woman to another: if you sponsor or recruit someone and you see key positive attributes and potential in them, tell them!  You could be making a *big* difference to someone's life by telling them what potential you see in them and often it can take someone else to make you look at yourself differently.  You don't know how long it has been since they had a compliment paid to them and you may just make their day and begin to nurture a driving force within them that they didn't know they had. It's a small step like this that can be life changing to another.

## Creating self-belief

If you are someone who lacks confidence, then I hope the following tips helps you to perceive yourself in a different light. Look at all your core competencies, make a 'What am I good at' list, review this list, add to it, feel confident reading it and feel good about yourself and learn to grow stronger within yourself. You may be a good organiser, a good listener, great with time management, good with numbers, great at networking and talking to people. List *everything* down.  Begin today to feel like the business woman you are. You have to go there in the mind first before the body follows. You have taken the action by joining a Direct Selling company to be an entrepreneur, to step away from the 90% who prefer to be in a dead end job. You are controlling your own destiny by embracing your entrepreneurial side.

Self-belief also comes through learning to do something well, so persevere with the company that you're involved with and get really 'involved' with what you're doing; put yourself forward for events, widen your comfort zone, attend trainings, meet more people, really engage yourself and get really 'stuck in' and this will really boost your self-esteem and confidence levels as you start to become an expert within your field. You'll always have a supportive upline there for you too so you're never on your own. Engage in personal development – read more and take the time to become better; if you become a better person, more strong and confident, then you'll go further. This is self-empowerment and you all have it within you to become better and stronger than you were yesterday. There is so much out there in terms of personal development material so just tap into it. If you learn to believe in yourself then others will begin to believe in you.

## Things to avoid

One mistake I have made is to 'mother' my team; this may sound familiar to you. As women, we tend to do this. Often when I found a distributor struggling in my team, I would feel inclined to step in and want to solve the problem *for them* and to make their life easier, do it for them. It's in our womanly nature to care and try and help our team members as much as we can. Often we can do far too much for them and end up running around and exhausting ourselves trying to look after everyone! What I have learned is to get your team members to do things for themselves. We are there as leaders to provide guidance and if someone in your team chooses not to follow that guidance, then that is up to them. If you mother your team too much, you will become mentally exhausted. Look at your team as eaglets; what you need to learn to do is nudge 'the chicks' out of the nest and if they do start to fall i.e. make a mistake, you fly down like an eagle would and bring them back to the nest for a while. Let me expand on that for you. Show someone *how to do something*, such as present the business to a new prospect. Then let them try it by themselves. Don't be afraid to let go and don't always feel you have to hand-hold. This encourages independence, not co-dependence. Co-dependence leads to a team that cannot do anything unless you are there. So after giving some initial hands-on training, encourage your team members to go it alone and try things for themselves, and if they are struggling then you can take a rain check and step in. This can be misconstrued by others as 'leaving your team to it', however, in reality, it's about creating independence. You don't want a co-dependent team who can only run their business whilst you are with them. By being far too available you create co-dependence; you will create a far stronger business by breeding independence within your team. If you look at the successful distributors within your company, they have independent leaders within their organisation building their own business.

## In Direct Sales you're dealing with 'real' people

Direct Selling is not a corporate world. Within the corporate world, women and men assume roles, attitudes, demeanours and personas that may not be true reflection of who we really are and we act in a manner in which we *think* we ought to behave. Women and men behave in certain ways to retain our jobs, to fit in, to be heard, to be promoted, to win that contract, to stay ahead of our peers. The corporate world is *not* reality; pluck those people out of their jobs into a home working environment and the dynamics are *completely* different. Direct Selling is a world apart from that of the corporate. You are dealing with 'real' people. Why am I making this juxtaposition? Because in Direct Selling you're dealing with people within the *real world* who are not hiding behind a fancy title or a business suit and therefore it's important to understand that that your leadership style needs to adapt accordingly as women and men process information differently. You're not dealing with people who are suited and booted and working within a 'persona' that they *feel* they *need* to be in; in Direct Selling you're dealing with the true person, with reality.

I hope you find the following section particularly useful, taken from my own observations and highlighting how women and men process information and how best to communicate to build a better team.

## Direct Selling Women - how to deal with the men in your team

*"Act like a woman but think like a man."*
**Dolly Parton**

When recruiting men into our business, it's important to understand that men simply process information differently to the way women do. When men join Direct Selling, they see a system of making money; they usually are not in it for the social aspect and merely want the facts of how the money is made when you recruit them. As a woman when you are recruiting a man, stick to the point. When a man asks you a question, give him the straight answer, don't beat around the bush. When I recruit men, I will only talk about the systems in place to earn them money and exactly what they need to do in order to making the system work. I'm not superfluous with my style and I stay away from small talk. I keep my presentation succinct, factual and to the point. I don't talk about the social aspect, how fun it is, how many new people I've met, how many friends I've made, what my favourite products are (only give essential product knowledge that they need to gain sales). So my initial meeting is purely factual about how the money is made, what he needs to do and any benefits he is going to gain.

When dealing with questions, queries and issues from the men in your team, feel free to answer the question directly and don't deviate off the subject or elaborate in any way. Stay as factual as you can. If a man in your team has a question, he just wants the solution or the answer to that issue or problem. You don't necessarily have to labour the point and feel as though you need to get into a conversation. As women, when we deal with another woman, we tend to have a more conversational style. A man just wants an answer to his problem. You can afford to be more direct with your thoughts, what they need to do and where they can improve. Most men can usually accept what you've said, digest it and take action.

## Direct Selling Men and communicating with women in your team

*"Women are complex and subtle.*
*Men are simple and direct."*
**Brian Tracy**

Women are opposite in the sense that we are more conversational; a phone call about business can quickly turn into a social chat. We are more drawn to the social aspect of what Direct Sales can offer. So for the guys out there reading, take this into consideration. Often, when a woman in your team has a problem, she may want to chat about it; as a man you'll want to offer a solution and that will be the end of the conversation. However, women like to talk, so take the time to understand this. Without realising, women in your team can feel a little isolated, through no fault of your own, just a difference in communication style.

What men need to understand when recruiting women is that we like to be more social, we like to chat about things and driven more by our emotions. So it's advisable to adopt a more rounded approach and don't just remain factual. On your initial presentation, talk about the social aspect of the business more, fun and friendship and fantastic products. Learn to make conversation on initial meetings talk about her home, children, her job, her pets – this is how women interact with one another and this will help you to create more rapport. Learn to make 'friends' with your new distributor.

When dealing with issues, enquiries and problems, women like to talk about the issue in hand even if no solution arises; in her mind it's been alleviated, even if not solved. It's been shared and that's the main thing. Guys, this is how a woman deals with matters: if something happens, it could be something positive or not so positive, we will pick up the phone and want to talk about it. We like to share, even if there is no conclusion or something to resolve. The more approachable you can make yourself as an upline, the more you will hear from the women in your team and build a better and stronger working relationship. You can make someone feel a million times better just by listening and talking to her. I was once told by a male member of my team that he felt 'disengaged' but it doesn't matter; just learn to listen and understand that it is the way that women like to communicate and it can help you build a better working relationship and deem you more approachable as an upline.

## Constructive Criticism

At some point or another, you're going to have to correct the distributors within your team. Remember you're dealing with people in the real world, not in a shiny office where everyone is suited and booted in the heart of a bustling city. What you can get away with in a corporate sense, you definitely cannot in the world of Direct Sales.

As women, we can sometimes take constructive criticism more to heart than our male counterparts do and I talk from personal experience here as I've been guilty of doing this myself! What I have found through *hands-on experience* (and ladies, please don't take this point to heart) is that men can often be corrected and will move on. Women, on the other hand, can be corrected but may feel bad about it long after you've pointed it out. With women in my team, I use the build and break principle MUCH more than I would with a man and will usually disclaim my point before I begin by saying lots of things along the lines of, "Please don't take this to heart," or "This is not a personal attack on you," or "I'm still on your side, you're great at everything else but...," or "Please don't take this personally but..." I have learned this the hard way, believe me.

On the other hand, with men I will use the build and break principle but will not reassure so much before I offer my suggestions. This is all about learning to understand one another and getting the best out of your team.

This is certainly not a definitive guide and there is a plethora of information out there on the best way to deal with people. Men and women process and digest information differently which is why your leadership style should adapt accordingly.

A fantastic book I can recommend on this subject is *Why Men Don't Listen and Why Women Can't Read Maps* by Allan and Barbara Pease, world leaders in body language and behavioural differences between women and men. Bringing out the best in people is about learning to relate to others in a way in which *they* digest information and according to their personality type.

Masters within this industry have honed and perfected their people skills. If you want to rise to the top of your company, focus much attention in developing your people skills and learning to understand how different personality types and people should be treated. Learn to get good at this and you will start to see amazing results within your business. Remember, at the end of the day, people are our commodity in Direct Sales; get expert skills with people and you'll set yourself up for massive Direct Selling Success.

## To conclude...

Now you've read and are familiar with my 21 Keys to Direct Selling Success, including my Bonus Key, I hope this has really helped to open your mind, give you new ways to approach your business and team building, and offer exciting new strategies in building your future income. I certainly hope you've taken notes along the way too!

Remember you can look online for further information www.directsellingsuccess.co.uk

Here's to your success on the road to Direct Selling Success, and I wish you all the very best on your journey!